Buoyancy
A Memoir of Determination

Angelina Piazza

"We gain strength, and courage, and confidence by each experience in which we really stop to look fear in the face... we much do that which we think we cannot."

-Eleanor Roosevelt

CONTENTS

1 ITALY: THE FINAL VACATION

I planned to fly to Pisa on New Year's Eve. When I booked my ticket I didn't think of the NYC traffic or the fact that it would be winter. I had to hope that all the traffic for Times Square would be gone and that it would not snow or sleet or precipitate in any way that would cause a delay, or worse. I packed the day before and had some very full and potentially overweight bags. I had to bring over some Christmas presents from our parents and any other requests that my sisters had. My flight was in the evening so we left our house early in the afternoon. Thank God there was barely any traffic. We arrived with plenty of time to spare. My parents got temporary passes to be able to take me all the way through security and to the gate. It was a good thing because my flight kept getting switched to different gates. And not to one just down the way, but we were going to the complete opposite side of JFK, several times. I would have been left behind. At first it was fine because it gave us something to do besides sit around and eavesdrop on other people's conversations or try to figure out who was my potential future Italian husband but after the third gate reassignment I just wanted to get on the plane. On the way across the airport we stopped to get some snickity-snacks and I bought a journal because I stupidly forgot to pack one. My memory is touch-and-go sometimes thanks to all the medications I take, so I wanted to make sure that I had something that I could document my trip in. It was the final adventure before my life completely changed.

12.31.08 Wednesday Evening

Currently sittin' first class sippin' champagne (glamorous, yes) with no one next to me- how could it get better than that? I was waiting and waiting in the terminal gate (which was officially changed 4 times) and nervous to see if they had realized I was there and needing help and hoping Manu wasn't dead from being left home alone all day and night. We left at 11h30 to come to JFK, and if mom and dad are just leaving the airport now, they won't get home until after midnight- he has no food but does have a pee pad. Mick and Rose were playing Pictionary the last time I heard from them. Nothing like bringing in the New Year with a game of guessing. Surely they are making it more comedic than the average person. So here I am in fabulous first class waiting for the flight attendant to take my meal choice from a real menu. Who knew they had menus and choices on an airplane?! Wandering if Manu is dead and whether or not Mick and Rose will pick me up on time and where the television/movie console is in this class? Bon Voyage!

01.01.09 Thursday Evening

I've made it safe and sound! Luckily, no problems, minus the line-up of over 35 planes in front of mine waiting to take off. I would say first class seats are a bit overrated. Maybe it was just because my little body didn't fit right in those giant seats. I'd say I slept for one to two hours total. I watched two movies and neither were that good. I did watch one of my favorites as well. It was about the life of Edith Pilaf. What a sad life and story. I got a bit sick, probably from the champagne (good thing that little bathroom was so close by). I saw a lot of that room. Now we are off to a restaurant called Aqua al Due to celebrate Mick's 27th birthday. They are known for their blueberry steak.

01.02.09 Friday Afternoon

We slept in almost until noon today! That felt good- we were up almost to 2 in the morning. Last night we hopped on the bus to go downtown (about a ten minute ride) and went to a very cute steak restaurant (and I don't mean like what they have in the U.S. with our huge steakhouses). It's just a nice little spot. We had to wait outside a bit, but it is a lot warmer here (40 degrees-ish) than in the States. We sat at a table in the corner by the window and there for my amusement was a smart car parked right outside! Hilarious little car. I saw a convertible one too. They just crack me up. We had some of the restaurant's red table wine; it tasted woody and a bit like bananas. Rose got a delicious pasta with pumpkin sauce and we split a steak fillet with blueberry balsamic- filet al mirtillo. Sounds better in Italian, as most things do. After that we had a tasting of three desserts and coffee. On the way home we passed the teatro and saw some ballet performances coming up that we wanted to see- Giselle or Swan Lake. Fun, but we are probably going to be in Udine when they're playing. But we haven't decided for sure if we were going to able to visit the family in Udine because the train ride is very long (five hours) and expensive, not to mention the fact that I don't speak Italian and our family doesn't speak any English. But, they are family and they already know I am here and are expecting us, so it wouldn't be a good idea to back out. We'll see. We are planning on going to see some new apartments for Rose and Mick and get a puppy! I want to get some leather gloves and a leather jacket. I miss Manu already- how pathetic is that!? He's not even my dog! I haven't gone a night away from him since August, which sounds like something a mom would say about her baby. Oy vie. Last night, as we were trying to sleep, we had a little show for us outside the window. A couple fighting at two in the morning. It ended with a door slamming and the other person getting in their car and driving off. How exciting. I love a brawl on a Thursday in the wee hours of the morning. The lesson I learned from this was (drum roll, please) I NEED TO GET EARPLUGS. Once you start wearing them, you can't stop! We're going to go to SACI (one of the places Rose works) and the train station and other stuff. It's sunny out.

01.03.09 Saturday morning

Just got finished getting ready for the day. Let's just take a moment here to say how spoiled I am back home! I have to take the fastest shower EVER so that everyone else gets a hot one. And meanwhile, since we do not control the heat it's cold in the apartment so that makes wanting to take a shower even more! Plus, the towels shed so I have little black fuzzies in all my crevices and on my body. Oh well, such is life, so hard when you have black fuzzies. We had a fun time out and about, but what I'm most excited for is our tickets we got to see the BALLET! And, I got mine for free! We are going to see

Swan Lake at the Teatro Verdi. I am super excited. It's Monday night at 17h30. We are also getting our Ufizzi passes today for 40 euros which allows us to go into the museums for an unlimited amount of times for a year. It's worth it even if I don't use it after this trip because one time alone could end up being that much. Yesterday we went to Rose's studio downtown- it was at SACI. It was neat because they had an outdoor studio in the terrace and the kilns to fire the clay were outside. We picked up some pieces Rose made. One of them was for me- a clay box she made with the fleur de lis on it- she knows I love that symbol! After, we got a quick cappuccino in a little bar. There were some stands right outside the place (well, they are everywhere downtown) and I got a cute knit hat (made in China of course) for three euros, it's blue. They had some pashmina scarves there for five euros each. If I would buy twenty scarves it would cost me 100 euros which would be approximately $149.00. But if we sold those scarves for $20 each at mom's shop it would end up being $400 which would yield a $351 profit. Not too shabby! I think they would get suspicious though- not sure what one person would be doing bringing all those scarves back to the U.S. Next, we went to get our Ufizzi passes, but it was five minutes before they closed so they wouldn't give them to us. We walked around more in that area, the fake Davide in that piazza was covered because he was being cleaned. We went to a leather glove store and I got two pairs. They fit for the most part, but the fingers are still a bit too long. I wore the green ones last night and they definitely keep my fingers warmer than the knit ones I have. I want to return the others, but I'm not sure they'll let me. I thought I'd need both! I did that when I bought a $275 coat in Rome two years ago and still haven't worn it. We went to Zara

(I love this store) because here they have kid sizes but they don't have those sizes in the States. I found an awesome gray coat which I wanted because then you can't see the animal hairs! We had to fix the buttons a bit because of my boobs, but it works. And by we, I mean Rose. I also got some nice gray and brown tights and a pair of sweatpants. After all that we were very hungry; we wanted to get some pizza but it wasn't open yet, so we made a pit stop at a bar nearby and got some apperitivos and a little munchy- happy hour style! I wasn't feelin' the alcohol thing, so I just got a coke, which was four euros. But that made it taste better, let's just pretend. They put two straws in it, why two straws? It's fizzy enough with one, two is awkward and weird. We had some yummy tomatoes with mozzarella and pizza and a good time. Good thing I had my lactaid pills!

01.04.09 Sunday Evening

We saw two apartments today. Too tiny and too expensive. One was super cute with stucco walls and exposed ceiling beams but a small bathroom. You could sit on the toilet and take a shower at the same time. Perfect set up for me. After those we went to Galleria dell'Accademia and saw the real Davide (I had only seen the imitation one in piazza della Signoria). He has big hands and feet. You could see the rock and sling- I never realized it was the Biblical David that killed Goliath; I'm not sure why I never put that together before. After the Accademia we stopped to have lunch at a place called the Yellow Bar. I had zuppa di verdure. Basically, in English, veggie soup. It was wicked salty, but I had a craving to fill. After that, we were going to go to the Bargello (a sculpture museum with those of Michaelangelo, Raphaello, etc). We walked to the Pointe Vecchio and saw the river. We were on the itty-bitty sidewalk and half of my wheelchair fell off and I almost fell in the street with a car coming. It stopped, thankfully, and some lady and her twelve year old son came to try and help as I was falling over. I didn't get hurt. It felt like it happened in slow motion. I wouldn't want to do that again. After that incident we went to an old church called Santos Spirito- huge and beautiful. Next up was the bumpiest ride ever. I felt like I was going to fly right out of my chair, I was literally getting air! It gave me whiplash for sure. My doctor would not be happy with that scenario. Rose wanted to make a neck support for me to wear like the neck pillows that people wear on airplanes. No thank you. All of the bumpiness paid off because we went to this little hole-in-the-wall cafe called Hemmingway. It's specialty was in chocolate. I had an amazing fondue dessert, to die for. After stuffing our faces and bellies with as much chocolate as we could handle, we jumped on the bus and went home. However, the bus driver didn't wait long enough to let us off at our stop and we ended up going over (up and down) this steep bridge, in the dark, with the cars coming towards us so we were blinded by their lights. We made it. It was death-defying to say the least.

01.07.09 Wednesday Morning

I bought 12 postcards for only 5 euros. Now I just have to write them all and send them out. Let's hope I actually do it- not bring them back with me and put them in a box to be found years later like I always do. Today is a bit cloudy and rainy, but the past week it has been sunny every day, it's about time. Rose and Mick both go back to work today. Rose already left, I don't think she'll be home until after 20h00, long day of teaching English. I am with Mick today, she'll be teaching the little girls ballet. We don't go in for a few hours. It's nice to have the morning to relax and slowly get ready, but I wouldn't want to come home at 21h30 regularly. Then again, it's different here. I could like it, both ways have their pros and cons. I bought a book to read while I was here, "A Thousand Splendid Suns". It's a four hundred page book so I figured I wouldn't need to bring another but I was wrong. It was so good that I finished it last night. We were watching Don Corlione on television but it was in Italian so I wasn't able to understand, and that led me to reading. Now I'll be stuck with studying the tax stuff for the VITA program. I am supposed to have taken the test and gotten my certification by now, but that didn't happen. I was pretty excited, but they are so disorganized and don't communicate properly so that leaves me in the dark and is extremely frustrating (and demotivating- if that is even a word). I just need a plan, an idea of what is going on.

Yesterday was a holiday they call the Befana. Supposedly it is when an old witch goes around and gives out stocking full of presents. Like Christmas, only they give their stockings on January 6. It's kind of freaky. One Tabacci we went in was all decked out with a huge witch in the entryway and mini witches all over the place.

We decided to go to another city for the day. For only 6,50 euros each we took a bus to Siena. We left around 10h15. It took an hour and thirty minutes to get there, but we made two stops on the way so that prolonged it. We went by Chianti and some other wine regions/cities. Right when we got off the bus there was a lady dressed up in a witch costume for the holiday. Freaky! Luckily, she didn't come near me. Siena is very hilly and seems almost like it is enclosed. It was the bumpiest ride I have ever been on. The road was made of huge stones, which made it worse because my wheelchair kept getting stuck in the cracks. My front three inch wheels were not meant for that terrain. Whoever pushed me had to keep me tilted back almost the entire time. At one point, to get to the main piazza (town square) we had to go down an extremely steep hill. I was scared. I hate any type of amusement ride (even if it's made for little kids) and this felt like one. I could just picture myself falling face-forward out of my wheelchair and smashing my head on the stones and rolling down the hill uncontrollably. Like that scene in Princess Bride when they're rolling down the hill covered with snow. That is what was going through my mind.

Siena is known for their annual horse race (Palio di Siena). Every year they bring in dirt and make a track right in the center of town. The Piazza del Campo is now regarded as one of the most beautiful civic spaces in Europe. Each neighborhood (17 total) is represented; it's a huge ordeal. They compete for a printed flag with the Blessed Virgin Mary on it. Grown men cry over this race if they lose for their neighborhood. I saw a special about it one time on the National Geographic Channel. Pretty crazy. Rose mentioned, they even bring the horses into the churches for the priests to bless. Ridiculous. Their passion is evident here! We also went and saw the Duomo (main church of the town). It is very beautiful. It's hard to wrap my mind around the fact that it was built before my country was even founded! The guy in the booth collecting admittance fees let us in without having to pay. It's moments like that that make me feel okay to be in a wheelchair. The door of the church was made of clay. When you get really close to it you can see that each door has many little scenes carved into it. The floors were all very intricate portraits or pictures or designs. I think that it was all marble. It had all black and white columns and tall, tall ceilings. Outside, one area of the building was all a facade- the story goes that they were going to expand the church, but the the black plague came around and people were dying, running out of money, etc., so they never finished it, and now it is just a tall building wall.

I somehow hurt my shoulder a few days ago, it feels like it just popped out of the socket, but it became more painful as time went on. Yesterday it was so bad I couldn't make the pain go away, even just resting it killed. Going around in my wheelchair was so bumpy and made it hurt even more. It radiated to my neck. We had stopped at a little bar to warm up a bit while we were in Siena and it was hurting so badly that I started to get spasms in my back. I couldn't keep it together and started to cry. I never cry over pain unless it is really bad. The last time was after my arm surgery when the novacaine was wearing off and the nerves were reconnecting. I couldn't take any more pain medication because I had taken the maximum for that day. So, while we were at this bar, with tears in my eyes, I had Mick order me a shot of sambucca to take the edge off. It warmed me right up and helped to relax me almost immediately. Last night (Tuesday), it started feeling better, but now this morning it is throbbing again. It's very annoying.

When we got back to the bus station we went to Avis (the car rental place) but it wasn't open so we went home. We are trying to rent a car to go to Udine this weekend because we told the family we were coming to visit and the train is expensive and we would have to rely on them to pick us up so we wanted to just rent a car. The main problem is that we need an automatic vehicle (neither Mick nor Rose can drive a stick shift). Well, Mick says she can and just needs to practice. No thanks, let's just keep looking for an automatic one to rent.

When we got home we made yummy pasta with sauce. And by we I mean Rose and Mick. I helped by watching them and taste testing the cheese and wine. Then we watched a movie (and I read) and went to bed. That was our Tuesday.

Monday was pretty uneventful. We slept in, walked around, tried to rent a car, but they were out of automatic cars, bought our bus tickets to Siena, and went to the train station. We were looking to get tickets to Rome for when I fly home on the 17th. It's about 45 euros one way, so we are going to look into a bus fare.

We went to the Co Op and got some groceries and then went home to get ready for the ballet that night. Mick made a yummy chicken (which we almost didn't get to eat because it took so long to cook) and roasted potatoes and salad. We made it to the theater with plenty of time to spare. Our seats were pretty good but I had to stay seated in my wheelchair and behind a guy with a huge head so I kept having to move side to side to see. I thought it was a live orchestra that would be playing for the dancers, but was wrong. The dance company was from Moscow. For the most part they were very good but at times it seemed they didn't give it their all. But it was a sold out show. There was a wide variety of people- a lot more children than I expected. After the show we went to that Pazzo Pizza place again but this time for desserts. We went with a friend of Rose's and two of his friends that he knew from university. Everyone had a cheesecake, but I wasn't feeling it. I got this sweet liquor that you dip biscotti in. It was pretty good. So that was the start of the week in a nutshell.

01.08.09 Thursday Morning

Last night, as we were preparing dinner we started coming up with some proverbs. We were a bit tired from the long day we had so they are punchy... 1. If you see an elephant on top of a hill you should join him. 2. Sweatpants solve all problems. The first one we came up with was because we were talking about the earthquake that just happened in Lititz and how much Manu didn't react at all, which is odd because animals can tell when a natural disaster is about to happen (like with the tsunami in Asia: people said the day before it happened they saw all the elephants running to the top of the hills).

Today, I stayed at the apartment. This afternoon Mick is teaching nearby and then she has to take a train to a town called Prato to teach two classes for this evening. Rose had to go to the ceramics studio and help clean up and prepare for the next semester which starts Tuesday. She came home a bit ago and we had lunch and then she had to leave and go teach English. She will be done around 17h30. So I am just going to hang here in my pajamas and attempt to study my taxes stuff. But, I started a new book by John Grisham called "Playing for Pizza" and I am almost finished with it already. It's very interesting because it takes place in Parma, Italy, so it is neat to be in the same culture. It was funny because the other day as we were walking around we were wondering about the differences between an enoteca, trattoria, etc. Then, as I was reading the book they talked about it! So here is what I learned: an enoteca is a wine bar/bistro style restaurant, a trattoria is less formal than a ristorante and has casual service and lower prices and is sometimes famliy-style, an osteria is traditionally a dining room at an in, and a ristorante is elegant and expensive.

01.09.09 Friday

Mick didn't have to work but Rose did in the afternoon, so we actually got up at a decent hour (we have been sleeping in for sure, usually until 10 or 11 am). We stopped at a bar to get a quick bite to eat and a coffee. I also MAC-ed out 100 euros (which was gone in one day). Mick and I jumped on the bus to go look at another apartment and Rose met us there on her bike because she had to go to work later so it was easier to take it right away instead of having to go back home and get it. She beat us there. The apartment was all the way at the top of the building and too small. It didn't even have an oven, just a microwave. There was a spiral staircase to take up to the nice terrace which had a grill. After that we went to the Bargello museum. It was very cool there, the way they had it set up and displayed made it feel clean and not overcrowded. It is the oldest public building in Florence and was once a barracks and a prison. When I found out executions took place in the yard there I got the chills. We also were able to see the newly cleaned and restored David. After that we had a sandwich at a shop called Snack Bar Silvana. Rose left from there to go teach her class. Mick and I used the restroom there and the lights went out on me- I took too long I guess. It's bad enough going to the bathroom in public let alone when the lights aren't working. We headed to the Avis car rental afterwards to see if an automatic car was available for the weekend and the cost. They did have one and it was about 140 euros to rent it. In the end we decided not to go to Udine. With gas and not knowing where we were going it just seemed too overwhelming. We walked through the market in San Lorenzo and I bought more leather goods, I hope those cows were treated properly. This time it was a nice red leather purse. The original price on it was 85 euros, but the old guy sold it to me for 45 euros. He probably still doubled his profit. We headed home and went to Vino Spuso to get our wine bottles filled. I tried a sweet white wine that tasted like grapes right off the vine. We bought a bottle of that and had three other bottles filled with red wine. The total for four bottles filled was only 12 euros! The place is owned by a family and a guy our age named Tommy was there. He gave Mick his number and invited us to a wine bar called Zona 15. He was good looking. His dad was there working too and he was very sweet. When we got back to the apartment we prepped it for our dinner party we were having that night. We had eight people crammed around the table. It was a lot of fun and lots of laughing. Mick made an awesome tiramisu for dessert and Rose and Mick made a lasagna for our main course. We were all together until one in the morning exchanging lame jokes that would get lost in translation (English, Spanish, and Italian). Then it moved into childhood stories. Those are always entertaining, even the ones we have told and heard a million times. It was definitely a great time.

01.10.09 Saturday

We slept in very late. Mick continued their apartment search while Rose and I went downtown to see the Palazzo Medici Riccardi. It was very interesting and they had a restored painting by Raphaelo of Mary and baby Jesus which was amazing. They had to restore it because it was ripped up and faded. They were able to make it look brand spankin' new. It was like how they re-release old kids movies in high definition with better sound quality. The exhibition was very well done, the way it set you up to see the final piece was perfect. We wandered around the palazzo and found an elevator to go up to the chapel that has the fresco of the magi. But we couldn't get anywhere in that elevator- it made no sense because each level it opened to was in-between actual floors and only was stairs to go up or down. Basically it was the elevator to the stair landings, but once you got there if you're in a wheelchair you can't go anywhere else. We finally figured out where to go and it didn't involve the elevator. Thank goodness I am compact and portable! Rose just hoisted me up the stairs and it was well worth all the hassle. The chapel was amazing. The whole room was a painting. We stood in awe. You don't see things like that everyday. When we left the palazzo we headed over to San Marco but ended up having to skip that because there was some sort of protest and a huge crowd was walking in the middle of the street and then there was another huge crowd just standing in the piazza, all chanting something we couldn't understand. There were some signs about freeing Palastine. It was pretty scary; there was definitely unease in the air. We got out of that scene and ended up in the Santisimmo Annunziato, a church where you could go in and view it like a museum or go to mass, take your pick. Mick met up with us there and we decided to swap dessert and dinner and went to Le Parigine for some delicious gelato even though it was cold enough outside to see your breath! I decided on dark chocolate and hazelnut. The chocolate was so rich tasting I couldn't even finish it. But that isn't anything out of the ordinary, I rarely finish any food. We ventured on over to get bus tickets to San Gimingnano for the next day. They only cost 12 euros round-trip. It took me so long to say the town's name correctly. I had to repeat it over and over for the rest of the night and on our way there. After we bought our tickets we went back home to eat a delicious dinner Mick made...spicy chicken soup! After eating we got ready to spend a night out on the town. We left around 22h to go to Tommy's wine bar, Zona 15. We had to go down some creepy and dark alley-streets and started to second guess going there. We finally found the place and when we walked in it was completely empty. And we thought we were getting a late start to our night! It was okay though, it turns out he actually works there (we thought he was playing in a jazz band). Talk about lost in translation. We just stayed for an hour, long enough to have one drink. Next we went to a small bar called Naima. Rose and Mick knew the guy who ran it so we knew it would be a better atmosphere with more than five people there. We each had a mojito and they were good- this is where we were able to start to relax that evening! We were there for a good amount of time. We had a table in the corner where we could see all the people and then some people Mick and Rose knew came up to chat with us. Last stop of the night was a nightclub called Twice. It was a dance techno style, something not often found in the States! We had a great time. I love techno, so it was fun. It was packed so I couldn't just dance on the floor. We found a short, empty table and Rose stuck me up there to dance with me. Yes, I was dancing on a table. It was for safety! Some random dorky guy came up to Rose and me and asked Mick if she could take a picture of us. I knew he just thought I was some sort of amusement to him, but I was in a good mood and played along with him, lucky for him. We didn't stay long because it was getting too crowded. We walked back to the apartment and got there around 1h30. We had to get up and be at the bus station by 10h the next day. I thought we could do it but my stomach decided otherwise.

01.11.09 Sunday Evening

This morning I woke up and puked twice. I might as well have just stayed on the toilet. Everything was spinning and I was so sick and nauseous. I guess those warnings on my medicine bottles aren't just there for looks. Do not take with alcohol really does have some weight to it. After I puked my brains out I stayed in bed until noon. I didn't start to feel better until after 14h. We didn't get to go to San Gimignano. But, we had fun last night and it was nice just to be home and relax all day with my sisters. I could catch up and start another book that Rose brought home from her school called "Behind the Scenes at the Museum" by Kate Atkinson. So far so good. I hope I can finish it before I have to leave to go back home to PA.

01.12.09 Monday Evening

Wow, I can't believe I have been here for twelve days already. That's sad because it means I only have 5 days left. We went and saw another apartment today and then went to a pasticceria called Marcello. The weather was so beautiful today, it was in the mid 40s. Not bad for January! Mick and I went to the Palazzo Piti-there is a museum of modern art we wanted to see there. Also the Boboli Gardens. We walked most of the way because it was so good to be outside and get fresh air. Then we jumped on one of the mini buses for only five minutes and there we were. We got our free tickets, thanks to the Ufizzi pass, then headed on in. Surprisingly there was an elevator to get to the modern art museum. However, when we got to the right level, the signs all pointed to a closed door. The Museum of Modern Art was closed today! Not cool. So we went to the gardens which was nice because it wasn't too cold out. It was slightly difficult to get around because of the gravel, but we ended up finding one section where you walk along a path that is covered by trees that arch over you. It was so fairytale-like. When you get to the end of one part you see there are several others that are all connecting to the midpoint. That would be a very nice place to go to often, once the weather gets warmer. It is definitely better than Longwood Gardens. As we were walking around we saw four cats! Mick said they are for the grounds there and they keep the mice away. We also noticed how fat they were and then saw a bowl of food out on the porch of one of the buildings on the grounds. We had to use the bathroom and there was a little building that said it was handicapped accessible, but we had to go down a small flight of stairs to get there. I would think that makes it not accessible? The actual bathroom itself was accessible- huge in fact. I guess their ideas of accessibility are different, which is fine for me as long as I have someone with me to be dependent upon, but is not something I want all of the time. We walked around for a bit and as we were leaving we saw a cat hanging in the fountain just drinking some water. It struck me as funny to see this cat chillin' in the fountain so old and preserved and revered as an amazing piece of work, protected from evil- it was very amusing. After we left we walked around and looked in the windows of the shops. I liked that area of the city, smaller and older feeling, more quaint. We got some sandwiches at a sandwich shop. We went to one of the bridges that cross over the Ponte Vecchio and sat there and ate our sandwiches in the sunshine. It was nice until all the teenagers came out of their school and congregated right where we were. Let's just say teenagers act the same no matter where in the world they are. When we were done eating we jumped on the bus and went back to the apartment. I read for a bit and took a nap which was very much needed. Mick had to go to work and teach at dance class so that was what I did while she was away. She came home for about an hour and a half between classes and we had some eggs and fresh mozzarella cheese balls. I could eat those things all day and night. Then she went back to teach another class. When she got back, we left to go meet Rose downtown for dinner. We went to an osteria called Osteria del Gatto e la Volpe. They know the guys that work there so it was fun. I had been to this restaurant two years ago with Rose and some other friends. I had the most delicious Alfredo sauce on my pasta. Not too cheesy, just deliciously rich! Yum. We ate and hung around there for a while. The one waiter played a trick on me. He was giving me a coffee but then acted like he was going to spill it all over me. I reacted, then saw that it was empty. Rose told him to do it. When we were finished it was too late to take the bus so we walked home.

01.13.09 Tuesday Evening

Today we got to sleep in and have lunch together here at the apartment. Mick made French toast! It was delicious of course, almost motivates me to want to start cooking, almost. I went off with Rose to her class she works with at SACI (Studio Art Centers International), an art school in Florence. The professor that Rose works with, Lisa Nocentini, is an artist, and has her works published in Ceramics Monthly and has taught at SACI since 1990. I visited the SACI website and it had a lot of resources for information on Florence. One amazing thing

I learned is that it contains more great artworks per square foot than any other city in the world. After we were done class we tried to go to the San Marco Church but it was closed. Last time we went there, there was a protest so it seems to me that I won't be seeing anything in that church! We went to a café and I tried their hot chocolate, which is basically just melted chocolate. The first few sips were delicious but after that forget about it-they gave a huge teacups worth! I paid for that later. Note to self: my stomach wants nothing to do with Italy's hot chocolate. We got a few groceries after that and headed home. Rose had to teach a private English lesson and Mick was in Prato teaching dance and then came home and made dinner.

01.14.09 Wednesday Morning

I did not sleep well at all last night, Mick couldn't either. It was weird. We went to bed at midnight and just tossed and turned. I just read until three in the morning. It didn't help that the street cleaners were out there for two hours making the loudest noises ever, shining their bright lights in the windows. I even tried the milk drinking technique! At least I got pretty far in my book- I have to finish it before I go. I haven't done any more of my tax preparation stuff, I am considering not doing it now. It is too disorganized and I can't get the info or answers I need. Plus, I can't attend the state/local class on Saturday because of a wedding I have to go to. We will see what happens. This morning it's raining, which is yucky. Rose and Mick went to go see an apartment and came back in bad moods. They had a huge argument. I stayed out of it- a roomie fight. Then I found out I messed up all the pictures that we have taken and now none of them can be printed because I saved over the originals and deleted them off the camera. Today has not been a good day so far. It is now 13h22 so there is still time to turn it around. Rose already went to work and Mick doesn't have to go in for a few hours I guess. She's just hanging around here on the computer. We were going to go back to the Palazzo Piti to the Museum of Modern Art because it's open today, but I honestly don't feel like doing anything right now. It's just one of those days you want to get over with and move on. My shoulder is killing me and my stomach acid is in my throat. I am in the bedroom right now and the light in here keeps flickering and is driving me nuts, but I am too lazy to go into the living room and I don't feel like asking Mick to move over on the couch she is sprawled out on. Tonight one of Rose's friends is coming over to make us dinner- pasta with salmon. I'm not too fond of this kid. But I guess he's a nice guy in general, so there's really no reason to not like him, but he just gets under my skin. It's like he's trying way too hard for us to accept him but I just don't particularly click with him or his personality. Mick went to get our tickets to Rome for Saturday. We leave at 9h30 to get there by noon with only one transfer. I think it ended up being about 130 euros for us three which I put on my credit card. Racking it up. I don't even want to think about the status of my finances and what I need to do when I get back. And on top of that I'll have to work on mom's shop and her taxes and doctor appointments and going back to work and blah blah blah. I don't even want to go to the wedding on Saturday. I am in a bad mood along with everyone else I guess. I'm going to pick up my crap and read some more. Maybe some hot tea will help.

01.15.09 Thursday Afternoon

Okay, so things panned out yesterday. I stayed home and finished my book and went online and hung out. Rose's friend came over around 19h30 to start cooking dinner for us. It ended up being pretty good, especially since I don't like pasta and seafood mixed. Rose got home around 20h and Mick around 20h30. We had some good fizzy white wine and Rose said it was only two or three euros for one bottle. We can't find wine of that quality for that cheap in the States for sure. Everyone was happy and kind to one another which was good, a change from earlier in the morning. We had a good time. We were talking and talking about the book they want me to write and how one of the chapters will be titled "Getting Along With Idiots" and how it will have stories about my horrors with a coworker. As we talked Rose's friend just fell asleep on the couch. We all ended up going to bed by 23h which is the earliest we've gone to bed since I've been here. We ended the bad morning with a fun night, and that is the beauty of sisters- we can be so mad at each other one moment and laughing with one another the next. And the picture disaster I created only affected 2 of them not, all 140 or however many there were. I uploaded those and placed an order, so they should have those to me by next week in the mail. I only ordered 14 because I know when I go back to work everyone will be asking about it and I will be able to show them a glimpse. I need to come prepared with a few moments to share with them, which I am not looking forward to. I don't want to be asked over and over the same "how was your vacation?" And I know they will want to know details and hear the exciting moments and all that because they are nosy and like to live through other people because they never travel. It's true. I will make a list of what I want to share: dinner for Mick's birthday (steak with blueberries and balsamic vinegar), going around looking at apartments, seeing Michelangelo's Davide in l'Acadamia, going to Siena where they have the horse races in the square, going in with Mick to work and watching her teach little girls ballet, going in with Rose to join in her English class of 14-year-olds, and how the weather was in the high 30s in mid-40s, it only rained two times, getting first class on the ride over, and that I got to see Swan Lake. Those should be enough for them. This morning we got up around 10h00 and had breakfast. I had tea and a piece of panetoni and after that I became very nauseated. My heart was racing. Rose and I planned on going downtown to the market to get some dried fruit. Since I felt sick I thought I would be okay once I got outside and got some fresh air. We made it to the bus stop, but I actually started feeling worse, so I asked her to take me back. I just made it to the bathroom and puked my guts out! Good thing I didn't go on the bus because that would have been a bad scene. Throwing up all over a busy bus with people looking at you. I felt like a new person after that! I just laid down for a few moments and we didn't end up going downtown. Rose was able to make a few more inquiries about apartments and scheduled two appointments to see some. We are going to go look at one tonight. I went with Rose to her English teaching job at the London school. I am in her second one now. It is a one-on-one lesson with a 14-year-old girl who doesn't try or do her homework so it's a bit frustrating. But before this one, she had a whole group of 10-year-olds that were very good in English. We went over professions and will, won't, may, maybe. It was a good class; Rose was very good at including everyone in doing a mix of activities to keep things exciting, fresh, and on track. So, now I am just waiting for her to be done teaching this student and then

I think we are done here. I believe we are going to be going out to a club or something tonight. Mick had class in Prato this evening and will be back around 20h00. Tomorrow I don't think she has any classes. We are going to go to San Gimingnano. My last day in Italia. Saturday morning at 9h30 we will be boarding a train on our way to Rome and will be arriving at the airport at noon and then I will be boarding a plane at 14h30 and I'll arrive in New York City eight hours later. Good thing I have Sunday and Monday to recover before I have to go back to work on Tuesday.

01.17.09 Saturday Afternoon

I am wicked hungry right now and waiting for the plane to take off. Sadly, I did not make the cut to first class. I am in an aisle seat which is good, and there is an empty seat next to me and the window seat is occupied by an Italian man. We are heading down the runway now. Getting here was pretty easy, but we had a mini adventure. We had to be at the Florence train station by 9h00 to get our 9h33 train, but we wanted to have special handicap seating so we had to go early to ask for that. As we left the apartment a bit late, we had to run to catch the bus to the station and almost missed it. Then, about two minutes into the ride I hear some noise, turn and see a lady on the floor of the bus! She had hit her head and completely passed out. Rose helped sit her up and gave her water. The bus driver stopped and was blocking the road so all the cars behind were honking and getting all bent out of shape. We ended up getting off the bus and walking the rest of the way to the train station. And by walking I mean running. We made it in time for the train, thank goodness, but the guy we talked to in the disabled help office was mad at us for not being there an hour early to get help on the train. He said we couldn't sit together so Mick ended up in another cabin. Rose and I got on with the chairlift and were put in first class. No one was in there except us. That guy in the disabled office did not know what he was talking about. We thought maybe we'd make some stops along the way and the cabin would fill up, but then the ticket lady came and Rose mentioned to her that Mick was in the other cabin and the ticket lady told us that she could come up because we weren't picking anyone else up. What in the world. Rose went back and got her and we had that whole caboose to ourselves. It was from 9h33 to 11h10 so it was very fast. And since it was first class we got a free drink of choice (I had tea) and some little cookies and candies for free. Once we got to the train station in Rome they met us at the train door with the chairlift and kept me in it all the way to the next train. I looked like an animal in its cage and Rose and Mick only made it worse by growling at me. We had to take a short 15 to 20 minute ride to the airport. It brought us right there, very convenient. We got there a bit before 13h00 and discovered the flight boarded at 1h30 which was cutting it close. Now the plane is flying high in the sky and the sun is shining bright. My legs are hurting already, especially my little muscle belly on my left leg which is aching and feels like it wants to pop right out. I don't know how I am going to move around on the seat. Oh well, one step at a time. My ears need to pop already! It was sad saying goodbye to Rose and Mick, but it was so worth it all. Last night we had dinner at home and they made some delicious chicken noodle soup and eggplant parmesan. We had a few friends over to join in on dinner and had a good time. We went to bed around midnight. Mick and I did end up going to the little town called San Gimignano. It was okay, everything seemed to be closed for the holiday which lasts until March! We walked around the city walls, which had amazing views, had lunch and went back to Florence. We got back at 17h00. Well, I am going to try and get at least a bit more situated in this seat, but who knows how that will work. They just mentioned something about serving lunch... YAY! I hope it's chicken. Delicious. With some carrots and green beans.

01.18.09 Sunday Morning

We landed nine hours later at 17h50 in JFK airport and dad made some good time on the way home. We got here within 2 1/2 hours, crazy! I just passed out in the backseat with my pillow and blanket that mom brought for me. The rest of the flight was okay. I was able to get up and stretch my legs and go to the bathroom a few times. I wasn't able to fall asleep though. I ended up watching three movies and the one in Italian with English subtitles ended up being my favorite. It gave me something to do and kept me occupied. Last night, when I got home, mom and dad said they had a surprise for me in the room, something they had been working on for the two weeks while I was in Italy. I opened my bedroom door and it was a whole new room! They took everything out, repainted (blue green walls with one yellow accent wall), put up a beautiful hand painted ceiling light globe, a new bed spread, and a comfy reading chair. And the best part... a beautiful new closet and built-in shelf that my uncle Steve and dad built. It is amazing and has French doors to open the closet and a light and a hamper and shelving. It is so wonderful. I think this was the best gift ever and makes me happy not to leave for some time. What a great ending to my last vacation.

2 FIRST TIME IS NOT A CHARM

My name is Angelina Piazza. I was born in New Jersey on September 10, 1984. My parents are John and Lori. My dad's real name isn't John, it's Dario. Only my mom and his family call him Dario. You know my mom is mad at him when she calls him John. They both grew up in Massachusetts and met in college. My dad is an engineer at a nuclear power plant. My mom is a mom and an artist.

I have two sisters...I'm stuck in the middle. Michelina is 2 years older and Rose is 18 months younger. We recently obtained our Italian citizenship, making us dual citizens of Italy and the United States. Rose lives in Florence, Italy. When we were younger we fought a lot, but now we're all in our mid-twenties and I consider them to be my best friends. I would be miserable without them. We love to laugh together and always look out for each other and would do anything for each another. At 3 years old, Mick pooped on the porch. Rose was 8 or so when she vacuumed Mick's hair. We made it an exciting childhood. I wouldn't change one thing about it.

Although, sometimes I wish I had a brother (mostly just so that I could marry one of his good-looking friends).

I'm 3 foot 10 inches tall. I usually have my hair short-it's easier, but expensive to keep up. My eyes change color from blue to green and in-between. Mick got me hooked on threading my eyebrows and mustache (I am Italian, I do have annoying lip hairs). My teeth are the most expensive part of my body. I've lost count of how many crowns have been put in my mouth. The most recent were the front 4 teeth that were capped in porcelain. I hate my feet. They're extremely flat and on my right foot my middle toe is the longest. Some people refer to it as THE TOE. I'm very embarrassed of my feet and rarely wear open shoes/sandals. My knees knock together and I have very little muscle in my legs. There are a lot of white scars on my legs from surgeries. My elbows are odd; they look swollen. I'm barrel-chested and have a hard time finding shirts to fit over my boobs. I have a tattoo on my left upper arm. I had my belly button pierced in college. I only wore a ring in it for a year. I am lactose intolerant. I was right-handed, but after the most recent surgery I had to start doing things left-handed.

I have a high voice; on the phone people think I am a little kid. I am anal. I like to have the channel changer when we watch television. I don't like messes but don't mind making one. I have been called feisty. I love to read. I'm a closet painter and can't part with my paintings. I like to be in the loop. My observation skills are well developed. I love getting mail. I love reading the Sunday newspaper and cutting coupons and completing the crossword and sudoku in the games section. My aunt and uncle come over frequently and we play cards and eat food and have lots of laughs. I am very picky about pillows. If it's not the right squishy-ness I will just sleep without one. I don't have a favorite color; I like neutrals.

I will eat anything my mom or sisters cook. I typically hate eating in restaurants, but if there is outdoor seating I will go without complaint. I prefer to read memoirs, but a corny fiction now and then is okay by me. I love going to see the orchestra or opera. I'm not a big fan of going to see a movie in the theaters. I love all music except rock and country. Techno, rap, and classical music top my charts. I like going to art museums, they make me feel intelligent. I can't stand ignorant people. There is no excuse. I hate when I see people spitting in public or swearing when there are little kids around.

I live at my parents house with Mick and her daughter Giovanna. Ours is a unique and convenient little town. Every 2nd Friday all the shops stay open late and there's entertainment and lots of people milling around. I love that I'm able to ride my wheelchair to the library. I volunteered there for a summer during high school. I wish that I could take Manu in with me. Since he can't go into the library I take him on walks all around the neighborhood, usually at least one mile a day. Random people will stop and ask if I'm the girl that takes the little dog on walks in my wheelchair. I guess that makes me somewhat famous. Woo-hoo. Sometimes, I don't pick his poop up like I'm supposed to (by law). I'm afraid I'll fall over and won't be able to get up. Stranded. Like that old lady in the commercial that screams "I've fallen and can't get up!" and uses her necklace button thing to that call for help.

In September of 2008 I turned twenty-four. I told myself this was going to be a fabulous year. I wanted to make sure of it. It was a few weeks after I had the arm surgery that I was celebrating my birthday. I was healing well, but it was a lot more painful than I imagined. It was an intense procedure. A tendon in my wrist was removed and placed into my elbow. Then my ulnar nerve was relocated. The nerve pain was horrible. I can tolerate pain pretty well, but this was a whole different ballgame. I went through physical therapy and worked hard to get it functioning.

I went back to work after six weeks of short term disability. At the time I was working in the Human Resources department. I later found an analyst position. They thought I was a perfect fit and agreed to promoting me. I had already planned a two week vacation over the holiday (New Years) and they were fine with that and we set a date after that to start. The trip to visit my sisters in Florence, Italy was another thing I was planning to make my 24th year amazing.

First I was promoted and next up would be a memorable time in Italy. What else was in store for me?

Originally, this surgeon was going to be working at the hospital that I normally go to in Hershey. My orthopedic doctor that I had been seeing for many years was moving to another state. I wasn't sad about that one bit, he was a self absorbed jerk. He didn't listen to what I told him and didn't monitor me properly. At one point, during college, my hips were hurting me so badly that no matter what I did or didn't do they were constantly in pain so much so that it was distracting. It was affecting my quality of living for sure and I was taking a lot of pain medicine just so I could sit through class or complete my assignments or hang out with friends or go to sleep. I would tell my orthopedic doctor and he would never have a solution and wouldn't even send me to get x-rays to make sure everything was okay. I mentioned all of this to my regular visit with my rheumatologist and she immediately sent me to get the x-rays which told her that I needed something done as soon as possible. She didn't know how I was even walking with those as bad as they were. We skipped going back to my orthopedic surgeon and went straight to a hip replacement specialist. I don't think I ever took my orthopedic doctor seriously after that. How could he be so neglectful? They tend to fall into two categories: aggressive and daring or conservative and slow to do anything risky. I think that he was just afraid to even touch me let alone do a joint replacement on a patient that had a disorder he had never worked with before.

My rheumatologist informed me that the new doctor replacing my orthopedic surgeon was from Baltimore, had dwarfism, and worked with a lot of patients that had the MPS disorder. I thought this was huge. I was excited to finally have a surgeon who not only saw things on my eye level but who had worked with others affected by Morquio syndrome. My disorder is so rare and whenever I see a new doctor it's extremely frustrating to have to tell the whole story from the beginning and educate them on what I needed. My legs were really starting to go back to being crooked. Knock-kneed. They form an X shape. It's painful, but mainly I was hating how they looked. I wanted this doctor to fix me up. Fast forward a few months and he backed out of his contract with the hospital I regularly attended. I found out through a sticky note my rheumatologist stuck on some papers she had sent to me in the mail. I had a consultation with a different surgeon they ended up hiring and had a bad feeling about him. He wanted to do some major surgery that would involve several steps and take over a year to complete. Aggressive is what I like, but he was almost giddy about it, as if I were some experiment or shiny new object he would get to operate on. I decided to get a second opinion from the surgeon that nixed the position in Hershey.

I scheduled my appointment in Baltimore. It was a beautiful day and the drive down went smoothly. I came prepared with my updated list of medications and surgeries. They hadn't received the records from Hershey so I ended up getting some x-rays from head to toe. They weren't messing around. After we were finished with those we were sent back to a room that barely was big enough to fit three people in it. There was a huge gurney, chairs, and a desk just big enough for the keyboard. I didn't know where to go with my wheelchair. Awkward seating situation. The doctor first sent in his right-hand lady, Tracy. She did a physical evaluation. I had to tiptoe across the limited space, back and forth a few times. My balance tested, my reflexes checked, and range of motion analyzed. We went over my medications and former operations. She asked me what I was there for and how I wanted them to help me. I told her about how I heard of him through my rheumatologist and I knew this hospital had a great reputation. I wanted them to fix my legs. I wanted them straight. She took all of this down and left the room. It took a long time for her to go over it with the doctor before he came in. I knew it was taking a long time because I had practically memorized the screen-saver power point that kept going on a loop. They had all these pictures of different departments waving to show they are into the sanitizing your hands program. How obnoxious to watch over and over. Then the door opened and here he came walking in. I felt very uncomfortable and could feel my face flushing. I don't know why, but I am automatically like that when I'm around other people who are short statured. It makes me feel so embarrassed that I turn bright red like that but it happens, no matter how aware of it I am. I just hope that they don't notice and that I don't say anything idiotic. He seemed okay, kind of a self-absorbed and a major wise-ass, but I figured that he was able to act like that because he knew what he was doing and talking about. He made it sound like he worked with other Morquio syndrome patients. He asked me what I wanted with him and I went to explain but he kept interrupting and adding his input. I wish he would've just gotten to the point in the first place and not beat around the bush. He told me what I wanted wasn't going to happen after what he saw in my films.

3 GROWING UP BUT NOT TALL

When I was around 3 years old my mom noticed some odd things about my growth. I was in the lower percentile for height and weight, but she also thought my elbows and chest looked odd. She took me to a doctor and he told her not to worry about it - that she was just looking for something that wasn't there. She didn't stop there or give up. Next she tried a specialist. This doctor agreed that something was not right, but wasn't sure what was wrong and sent me to a geneticist to determine the culprit of my symptoms.

MPS (mucopolysaccharide) disease. Morquio syndrome type IVA. It's a genetic storage disease caused by the body's inability to produce certain enzymes needed to cut up keratin sulfate. Cell materials accumulate and cause progressive damage throughout the body. It's estimated that it can happen 1 in 200,000 live births in the United States. It was first discovered during 1929 in Montevideo, Uruguay and in Birmingham, England. Symptoms that we were told to watch for included abnormal heart and skeletal development, hyper mobile joints, knock-knees, bell shaped chest, short stature, large elbows, flat feet, thin teeth enamel, and corneal clouding. They monitored my growth and development.

When I was eight I had to get my first pair of glasses. They were half the size of my face. It was the early 90's so I guess it was the norm to have glasses that make you look like a nerd. Now I have a different opinion of glasses, I prefer to have them on actually, they make me look and feel smart. The selection has also improved greatly over the last twenty years.

My family moved to Pennsylvania when I was starting second grade. I don't remember if I was nervous about being around new people or if I thought I wouldn't make friends. My parents put my sisters and me into a private Christian school that went all the way to grade twelve. My mom went in with me during the first day and brought my most recent x-rays. She put them up in the window for everyone to see. She explained to my classmates about the MPS disorder and answered their questions. They all seemed to think it was pretty cool. I had no problem making friends. I was blessed not to have any issues with bullies or isolation because of my disorder. Kids have an amazing way of bypassing obstacles. My friends didn't ignore my issues, they just worked around them.

In second grade I got some girls in trouble because one wanted to give me a piggy back and so did the other. I picked one and the girl that was left out went crying to the teacher on recess duty. I think they were all banned from giving me piggy back rides after that. I eventually ended up hating recess. I was much happier when there was a reason we had to stay inside for recess because it was a lot more fun and we got to do quiet things like read a book or play a game. Once in a blue moon they'd have a movie for us, that was the best. Normally we would be forced outside (even if it was freezing) and we would play kickball or dodge ball or foursquare. I was the designated pitcher for kickball. All I had to do was make sure that the ball rolled to the kicker. After some time they figured out it was more about just rolling the ball (speed and spin actually did matter) so I was never picked or included anymore. I became a curb dweller. I liked it because I could observe and take everything in, but I hated it for the same reason- I could only watch.

One time during recess in the winter, as I sat shivering on the cold cement, a girl with some mental problems was walking behind me on the sidewalk and she turned to me and whacked me one with her foot. Thanks to the layers I had on it didn't hurt, but now it seemed I was attacked because I was allowed to sit there. The teacher on duty would yell at anyone if they sat down. I think the teacher had nothing better to do and that kept them busy. It was torture for those kids that were not athletic. My saving moment was when the whistle would blow. Finally, we could go back inside and get on with the day. That whistle created a lot of chaos; instantly a herd of sixty 9 and 10 year olds clamored to the same tiny spot. We had to line up in single file according to our grade, and fast. It was scary; no one wanted to be yelled at or left behind so it was always a mad dash. At one point I requested from the recess police to warn me ahead of time as to when they were going to blow the whistle so I could get there first at a reasonable pace without all those kids rushing and squashing me. I feel like I had a good schooling experience. No one made fun of me and I actually felt pretty normal for the most part. I tried to make the best of every situation.

I have my many moments of self pity and loathing. One of the first truly heartbreaking ones was when I finally realized I wasn't going to be able to play field hockey. I was in middle school. The coach felt badly for me and wanted to include me. She cut back a field hockey stick and made it the perfect height for me. I never actually tried to join the team, it was just fun to practice whacking the ball. I ended up playing the water girl role. I couldn't even do that. The huge water jugs were too heavy for me to fill and lift. And I needed help dragging them up and down the fields to wherever we were going to be playing. I just wanted to watch and ride the bus with the team and go out to eat at Wendy's on our away games. It was a way I could be involved. Then, for some reason, I was given the task of team manager. I had to keep track of the goals and fouls and roster. I had no clue how to play field hockey, let alone watch and record. I was too embarrassed to ask for help and just struggled through it. On the way home in the van once a few of the girls complained that I was doing a bad job and didn't know what I was doing. They didn't realize I was in the vehicle on the seat in front of them. They couldn't see me. I could feel my cheeks burning and my eyes stinging. I quit after that.

In 8th grade we took a field trip to Gettysburg, PA for several days. We slept in tents at a campground and ate by the fire. The way we toured around was riding our bikes. I had bought a new bike in anticipation for this trip; it was purple and had gears and shifts. I could barely turn the shift bar, but that didn't matter, I could stay in one gear I thought. The teachers humored me and let me take my bike along, but as soon as we approached our campground in our yellow bus bumping all over the place, I knew there was no chance that I would ride my bike anywhere around here. I was officially assigned to the school van that carried supplies and injured/sick students. It wasn't as bad as I thought; I really enjoyed when the driver zoomed by my sweaty classmates on their bikes going up a hill and screamed out the window, "PASSING" to them. When it started to downpour on our way to a battlefield I didn't mind being dry in the van. It ended up being a fun trip for the most part. I didn't get to bond with my classmates by biking behind or in front, but I could do that while in my tent with my best friends or during meals together or when watching one of the most boring movies ever: Gettysburg.

In 10th grade an amazing thing happened to me. This time my class was on a field trip to New York City for a week. We were going to all the typical tourist sights, but we also put in some time helping the homeless at the Bowery Mission. It was towards the end of our trip when we were all tired from sleeping in a church gymnasium and were also sick of each other. You can only handle being around a bunch of hormonal teens for so long (even if you're one of them). That day was a rainy one so everyone seemed to be in a funk. But we had to get up and get going to the Mission. When we arrived they took us on a tour. All I could remember thinking was, "How can anyone live this way?" It felt dirty and dark and hopeless. It smelled horrible and we soon found out that stench was what they would be eating for lunch that afternoon. They showed us where all the men slept. The cots were all lined up and each had a set of blankets and a lumpy old pillow. I imagined what kinds of creatures were growing in those things. The stairs they took us up and down were old and rickety. I felt like we were going to make them collapse by going up them at the same time, like there was a weight limit and we were getting very close to it. The next room on tour was their chapel. The only condition for the men there to receive food and a place to lay their heads was that they had to attend chapel. The Mission had its own Pastor that would try to touch these men that were closed and hardened from life's circumstances. They would try to give them peace of mind and heart and instill a new way of living. They didn't have to suffer or be living on the streets with no hope. The chapel was the only place at the Mission that felt okay. It reminded me of a Catholic church with all the wooden pews lined up with Bibles in the backs. After we served the men their lunch we prepared ourselves for their daily service. We sang some songs for them and then I was given the opportunity to speak about some of the obstacles I had overcome so far in my short life, and about the hope and faith surrounding me. They seemed to enjoy hearing from me, these tough and rough looking guys had some tears in their eyes by the end of it.

After we left the Mission we were off to the NBC Studio right near Times Square. I was unhappy because my friends were arguing over who had to push me in my wheelchair next. They were sick and tired of doing it and I wished they didn't have to. We were crossing through Rockafeller Center and could see the NBC building ahead. It was cold and I was ready to just get this tour over with and get going on the bus home. We entered the building and discovered that in order to get to the meeting point for our tour we had to go up a flight of stairs. One of my teachers told me to wait at the bottom of the stairs (where else did he expect me to go?) while he went to find someone to let them know about me and figure out what we needed to do next. I was thinking that my teachers were idiots and hadn't mentioned to the NBC tour coordinator that there was a student in a wheelchair; now NBC was unprepared and scrambling to accommodate me. My whole class was held up waiting around for me and the problems I felt like I was creating. It was humiliating. I didn't want it to be about me. I didn't want to be the person causing drama or ruining the trip. We only hung around for a few minutes, but it felt like an eternity. Everyone was impatiently asking what was going on and why we were waiting. All the answers had to do with me and the disruption I was causing because I was in my wheelchair.

Finally a staff person came over and escorted me to the back of the store past all of the odds and ends of merchandise they had in there- everything from mugs to bracelets to clothing. A small, hidden elevator took me up to the second floor. We went down a long hallway with pictures of different celebrities and their shows that have aired on NBC. There was a small set that looked like a news casting room where you could sit and get your picture taken as an anchor. There was also a Saturday Night Live cast cardboard cut out where you could put your head in a hole to join the cast. The employee took me to the top of the stairs that we were just waiting at the bottom of and asked me to wait there because my class would be up shortly. In the meantime I was checking my surroundings out and noticed the bulk candy section. The cool thing about it was that there was a section that had about twenty different M&M colors each in their own bin. I had never seen a turquoise or hot pink

M&M. I was hoping we would be able to shop after the tour because I wanted to get my hands on those.

An older man with white hair had appeared and called a few staff members over to him and was whispering to them secretively; I noticed that he pointed my way during their conversation. He then came over and asked my name, how I was, etc. Making small talk. He wished me a great time and was off. I felt excited and wasn't sure why. Normally, if some random old dude tried talking to me I would not engage in conversation, but I did. One of the employees standing with me asked if I knew who he was. I didn't. She informed me that he was the President of NBC Studios. I was shocked. He actually talked to me! I met the President of a huge corporation. I could not wait to tell my friends (who were still waiting at the bottom floor). I did not see what was coming next. Another employee came up to me and told me that the President wanted me to go on a shopping spree in the store and get whatever I wanted and however much I wanted all on him. I could not believe my ears. A team of employees whisked me away to begin my extravaganza. I skipped the lame tour and loaded up on some awesome goods. I made sure to hit up the candy section first. We went back to those sets I saw on the way upstairs and got some pictures and then went back down the elevator to the other level of the store. There were tall stuffed M&M candy toys. I picked one out for Rose and one for me even though I had no clue where I was going to put it or what I was going to do with it. One of the girls on staff jokingly asked if she could have one for her daughter and I said sure! Why not? There were also some very nice leather jackets with the NBC logo on the front and I gave two of those to the employees that were accompanying me on my spree. I picked out a teacup set, key chain, pens, book bag, and other things that you would find in a souvenir store. It had to have added up to at least $5000. I took the whole time that my classmates were on the tour and then some. We had to rush to the bus and load the bags and bags of NBC gear underneath. Everyone seemed excited and couldn't believe my story. It was a great way to end our trip to New York City.

One of the first classes I had in University was one that I wasn't even able to get to. My French class was in an older building on what seemed to be the second floor. I had to hope there was an elevator. The morning of class I drove my wheelchair across a catwalk and down a hallway so skinny that the chair had no room on either side. I had to go extra slow just so that I wouldn't crash into the concrete walls. I made it to the end and had to make a tight turn but right around the corner was where the classrooms started. I looked above the doors to read the classroom number and realized I wasn't going to be able to make it to mine. It was the next floor up and there was no elevator to get there.

I went back to my dorm room distraught over what to do. I was afraid my professor was going to think I was a bad student who skipped the first class and was therefore a slacker and would flunk me. I emailed her to let her know that I wasn't in class at that moment because I could not get to the room. Almost immediately she responded and indicated she had no problem with me missing that first session and that she was working on getting a new room that I could access easily. By the next class we were moved and I was able to attend.

The cafeteria was another issue for me in University. It was set up with about four different stations, all of which were self-serve. The only time anyone came out of the kitchen was to replace one of the tubs of food or to refill the condiments. All of the counters were above my reach and I couldn't even see the food they had set out. I had to have someone come with me every time I wanted to eat so that they could get a tray and fill it with whatever meal there was that day. I felt like I was using them just so that I could eat. It was either that or buy a bite from the little take-out place where they made the most unhealthy food imaginable, nothing that resembled a complete meal. They had your fried mozzarella sticks, cheesesteak subs, and quesadillas. I made sure to stash up on groceries and find housing with a kitchen so that I could just cook my own meals.

I took a semester to study abroad in France. One of the scariest experiences of my life. It was during my senior year and it seemed like a great idea at the time, but the night before I left for Paris I bawled my eyes out. I was hoping it would turn out to be something I didn't regret. It ended being an amazing adventure and there never was a dull moment.

The first night all of us students studying abroad stayed in a hotel together. I had used my power chair a lot that day so I decided to plug it in and charge it. I rolled my chair into the bathroom and plugged it into the outlet with the charger that the Medical Supplies Store sold to me with the fact that France had a different electricity conversion in mind. A few hours later I smelled something like melting and burning rubber. That was a bad sign. I opened the door to the bathroom to check on my wheelchair and it was smokey in there. The battery was ruined. It took a good two months to get it fixed and it still never worked the same again. I had to have my friends push me around in my manual chair.

I was staying in an apartment complex where for some reason they had what was considered their wheelchair accessible studio up on the fifth floor. The only thing accessible about this place was that it was huge. Unfortunately, the elevator was quite old and broke down a few times. For some odd reason it always was evening when it decided not to work. It was late evening when no one was working and couldn't come out to fix it until the next morning. One night it was broken and I was waiting for my friend to respond to my text message (I had run out of minutes so I wasn't even able to call her) when these older guys came up to see what was going on and if they could do anything. They even offered to carry me up to the fifth floor to my apartment. I kindly declined their offer and prayed that my friend would call me. She finally did and I ended up riding over to her host family's house in the dark and staying there for the night.

I don't know why, but I am ashamed to admit that I am very uncomfortable around other short people. And I don't mean little kids; I mean people of short stature. Why would I feel this way when I am one of them? I don't like to stick out or be stared at, so maybe that has something to do with it. But mainly, I think it is because I don't always see or think of myself as a little person, but when I see someone like me, it is a reminder of who I really am and how other people see me. Physical deformities are hard not to look at and wonder about.

I never wanted to go to those conferences where everyone gets together and hangs out, and are all people under five feet. I couldn't wrap my mind around why I never wanted to go and probably never will. It must be a pride thing. I just don't feel it necessary to go. My mom wanted me to go and was going to pay for it all as a

Christmas gift. I told her no. She doesn't understand why and if she doesn't than no one else will. That is like me asking you what your defect is and send you to a place where others have that similar problem for a weekend. Some people might actually find that encouraging and enlightening. It could be a way to vent to others that actually get it and know exactly how you feel and what you are going through. There are many pluses to these things, but they are not meant for everyone. I feel like a lot of people would judge me and think it is ridiculous for me to feel this way, but sometimes ignorance really is bliss.

I want to live my life and work around my disability, not have a disability which controls my life. I surround myself with people that treat me like an equal and think nothing of my height or arthritis or other issues. If I hung around those with similar disabilities as myself I think I could become very bitter and unable to cope when in the real world. We would talk about all of our horror stories, how we've been discriminated against, what we deserve and don't get, and so on. This is not the kind of thinking that I want in my life.

Both of my sisters were dancers. I danced for a very short period of time but couldn't keep up and had to stop. I could no longer point my flat feet or do jumps across the floor or stand long enough to take a barre lesson. I watched them from the audience. I was the family mascot cheering my team on.

Instead of sports, I ended up playing the violin, but I quit soon after because the teacher paid more attention to the other student (who never practiced and was horrible at learning it). Then, I moved on to piano. I couldn't even reach an octave with my fingers and my feet barely reached the pedals. I started after my younger sister had already been playing for a while and she was more of a natural at it than I was. That made me hate playing. I also resented playing because every year we had a recital and I always forgot my piece and would be so embarrassed in front of all those people waiting for me to finish my song. I made a deal with my parents that I would continue to take lessons and practice as long as I didn't have to perform. They agreed. I still liked the lessons because I was allowed to get out of class for them and if I did well enough I would earn points towards the goody bin which usually had some pretty awesome candy. I ended up playing piano for seven years. I still love the piano, but only listening to others, not actually playing. Recently, however, I found a melodica at a flea market . It is one fabulous instrument (a mini keyboard type thing that has a mouth piece you blow into and it sounds like you're sitting in Paris on a beautiful sunny day outside a cafe drinking a glass of wine and the music is just floating around you). I bought it of course. It was only $25 and when I looked up the value online it was as much as $200. I don't play it that often, but I do like the idea of it.

My extracurricular activity was going to doctor appointments. A lot of time my mom spent on me. She was always sacrificing for me. We had plenty of visits where we would wait a minimum of two hours to see the doctor and then he'd talk with us for fifteen minutes. She made it bearable. She would ask the doctor questions I wanted answers for but was too afraid to ask or she would speak up for me if something needed to be said. She wanted to make me feel as normal as possible. We would go to the cafeteria and she let me get whatever I wanted to munch on and drink. It usually ended up being soda and some sort of sweets. I loved getting strawberry

Mentos. Books were always a refuge for me. I had plenty of time in the waiting room so we usually brought a book. I liked to sit in the waiting room chairs and put my feet up on my wheelchair. The only downside to that was when they would finally call my name I felt like I had to rush and make sure that they knew I was coming and that I was just slow. Everyone watches you as you scramble because they have nothing else to do. No matter what, I would always get stares from the other patients. I would go to a pediatric clinic so all of the patients were under the age of eighteen. All kinds of illnesses and disorders would be in that waiting room. From someone with a broken foot that needed a surgery to someone strapped in a wheelchair with head support and no way of communicating except by groaning. The ones that couldn't talk or express themselves in a way that I was familiar with made me nervous. I wanted them to communicate about what was hurting or what they wanted to drink or which outfit to wear. It is always harder when you don't understand something or someone. It makes you feel like a failure because you are unable to help them or know for sure what they want and need.

Now that I am an adult and fully in charge of my self-care and preservation I have a whole system to keep my doctors in the loop. I see my physicians for many different things, but I make sure that I have all the basics covered. To some it might seem anal but it's my way of preparing the doctors so that they can see the foundation and build from there. I give them a packet that describes my disorder very thoroughly and explains what typically happens to a person who needs to be seen for Morquio. I have a list of my current medications and over-the-counter drugs that I take, a list of my most recently seen doctors and their specialty, and a list of my operations with dates and some explanations. When I hand the packet of documents over to the doctor I almost always get the same reaction of, "Oh! You've come prepared!". I simply don't want my time to be wasted, so why waste theirs?

4 CHANGE OF PLANS

The news was that I needed surgery to stabilize and possibly decompress my cervical (neck) and thoracic (mid-lower back) spine. This is a common procedure that needs to be done with patients that have Morquio. My back had the gibbous deformity. Also called kyphosis, an abnormal curvature of the spine. It was evident and monitored for a long time and now it was showing that it needed to be treated to prevent myelopathy (nerve damage) and respiratory problems. My neck needed a fusion due to the deteriorating vertebrae. He told me that it needed to be done immediately. I knew the neck was going to need to be done again eventually but not this soon. Plus, I never even thought about my back needing actual surgery to correct it. So, I was stunned. I went in for something completely different. It could be done all at once he told me. First, he would go in to fuse my neck with a wire and piece of cadaver (yes, dead people) bone. I'd have to wear a neck brace. Then, he'd straighten and stabilize my lower back with a rod and some screws. He was going to have someone else there in case it would also need some decompression. No brace needed for the back. I was glad he caught something like this but what bad timing. I was about to go in for surgery on my elbow to fix my ulnar nerve. That was scheduled for the next week in Philadelphia. I wouldn't be able to do both back to back and have enough time off of work to cover it. I told him about that surgery and he recommended that I cancel the arm surgery. I told him there was no way in hell I was going to do that. I had been suffering with that arm for a long time and wanted it to be fixed. The reason for him to advise against it was due to the fact that my neck was unstable to the point of it being extremely dangerous to put a tube down my throat if anything went wrong. I told him I was not even going under general anesthesia, just a nerve block on that arm and some happy drugs. I left knowing I was going through with my arm surgery and would see him again when I was healed from that. I couldn't decide if I liked this guy or not. His bedside manners sucked, but he definitely exuded confidence in performing this massive surgery on me and made it sound like it would be a piece of cake for him. I needed to hear from my mom what she thought about him and if she had gotten any bad vibes. I trust her instincts on that sort of thing. We went out to lunch after the appointment. I should have gone back into work for the rest of the day, but after hearing all that I knew I wouldn't have been able to concentrate. We ate salad on a pizza thing and I drank this amazing mojito, much needed.

My mom has great people reading skills and she was a good voice of reason, after all, I might have thought I was in an okay state-of-mind to determine what to do, but after hearing that the condition that my body is in right now is life-threatening, my judgment could have been a bit clouded. I think my mind went into a different mode and I just wanted to do whatever needed to be done as fast as it could be done. Another hiccup that would alter my ever-changing plans. I am a pro now after having to restructure my life after these surgeries. As they say, change is good. Yeah, okay. Go with the flow. Do what you have to do. Everything will work out in the end. All these phrases I tell myself, but now I feel like I've said them so much that they have become something I say more sarcastically than anything. Maybe more with a grain of salt. I mean, I do believe they hold some truth to them, but after hearing them over and over I can still feel myself wanting to just roll my eyes at the thought of them. It is more annoying when other people say them to me and then I have to give the expected response of yes, it's true. I want to say, how would you know? Sometimes I would rather nothing be said from others. On the other hand, I am human and I do need a support system. So, I can't be nasty and bitter all of the time, I would push everyone away and become completely unapproachable and miserable if I did that. And sometimes I wouldn't mind that, but only momentarily. Why is it so much easier to be so down and out and then it is a lot harder and way more work to be happy and satisfied? I know my one way of being okay and positive is to go out on my porch with the sun shining and sitting in my comfy chair sipping homemade iced tea. And it gets even better with company, especially company that can just sit with me and have a great time without having to constantly be doing or talking. I think those simple things are what help me not go insane.

I would schedule the surgery for April 29, 2009. I had several months until D-day. I would have to tell my new boss (I had only been working with for a few weeks) that I would be needing this surgery and would be out of service for four weeks. The thought of that conversation made me start to sweat. I'd have to wear lots of deodorant that day. At that point I was confident in the surgeon and what he was about to do. I had no qualms or reservations.

The last day of work before the surgery was a Friday. I had only been promoted to this analyst position three months ago, but we had already made some significant changes and procedures were different. I made sure everything was up-to-date and in order. The manual was all revised and ready. I boxed up some of my things to bring home with me that I thought I would use or that would die (my plants) in the next four weeks. I emptied out my snack and candy stash. That stuff took up most of the room. I'm a muncher need something to eat or drink always. It breaks up the monotony of working. I figured I wouldn't want to leave stuff that might rot and stink the place up. And the candy would be okay, but it should be consumed quickly so I brought that home for when the family got together to play cards. Since I worked right across the street from the Central Market I was constantly picking things up there and one of them was loose leaf tea. I had many little baggies of it in all different flavors. Chocolate mint was one of my favorites besides good 'ole Darjeeling. It looked like I just hit up my dealer for some marijuana. I had my tea strainer and teacup next to the baggies so no one would ask any questions. Next order of business were my plants. I only had a few, but they were my babies. I had managed to keep them alive for 3 months at that point. I thought they'd be taken care of better at home. My boss gave us the okay to go home early since we had just finished up an assignment that we had been working all week to complete. I went around and said my "see you later"s to everyone. My co-worker carried my boxes down to my car for me. I made sure to leave some things in my cubicle to remind them of me when they walked by. My name plate was visible to all, my radio clock, my pen holder (made by Rose), and a picture of my family. I parked my power wheelchair near my cubicle near their mailboxes. That thing was huge and hard to miss so I knew that I'd be on their mind frequently, whether they liked it or not. Let's just hope no one would figure out how to turn it on and go for a joy ride. For some reason when guys see the big power chair just sitting there they automatically go into man-mode and want to jump in the seat and zoom all around. News flash: that chair is probably more expensive than your car and is NOT a toy and if it breaks then I am screwed having to wait for it to be fixed. I made sure I put the breaks on and the speed was adjusted to its slowest level possible. Last thing I said to my boss on my way out was, "See you in four weeks!"..

We left the house before it was even light out. Running late, as usual. While riding in the back seat I could feel my stomach turning. Partially because I wasn't allowed to take any medicines and wasn't to eat or drink that morning and the other was due to nerves. It wasn't an anxious nervousness. It felt like a peaceful calm before the storm. I kept telling myself is that this will all be over very soon. To this day I have to tell myself that. It's become a mantra of mine I guess you could say. It's a quiet hour and a half to Baltimore, straight down 83. Once we got to the hospital, Dad dropped Mom and me off at the main front doors. I wished we would've just found parking and then gone in all together. I guess Dad needed to get in one last cigarette while he could without being nagged for it. Now we had to wonder if he was going to be able to even find us. We had no clue where we were going. Luckily it was before the rush and it was pretty empty which meant more help for us if needed. For some reason they sent us to the pediatric check-in. We didn't question this because my surgeon mentioned that we would have a team of both pediatric and adult doctors to care for me. The nurses sent us to a corner of the room. Toys were everywhere and some annoying kid show was playing on the large flat screen television; I wonder whose salary didn't get boosted due to that television. There were a few other patients waiting for their surgery too. The nurses were acting a bit strange, we figured they didn't understand why a 24 year-old was in their area. My surgery time was getting closer and we still hadn't been addressed. This made me uneasy. The last thing I wanted was to miss my surgery time and then be sent home because they didn't know what to do with me or there wasn't enough time to do the surgery. Finally, somehow, we were rushed over to the adult surgery check-in. We were literally speed walking through the hallways. I had to hold on for dear life. Even the thresholds we went over seemed to bump me out of my chair a bit. Of all my surgeries, this was the fastest I had ever been admitted. One last bathroom break, changed into hospital gown, hooked up to the monitors, and poked with an IV. This all felt like it was done in ten minutes. No messin' around. Dad still wasn't there. They were about to wheel me away on the bed and he showed up. They must have started some relaxant drugs through my drip because I was getting very sleepy and feeling just fine.

The last thing I remember before going into the OR was seeing my surgeon sitting at the desk studying my x-rays. Words might have been exchanged, but I don't remember what was said. All I was thinking was he better get this done quickly and perfectly. I was still stuck on him doing both cervical and thoracic fusions at the same time. Other than that I was calming myself down by praying and telling myself that it'll be over sooner than I would realize. This was the same thought process I had developed before I went into any of my operations. I always would get nervous that I would wake up during surgery but they wouldn't know and I would feel everything they were doing but couldn't tell them. So, to counteract those thoughts I'd think of myself having dreams of me floating up in the clouds feeling fine and hanging with God.

As they rolled me into the room I kissed my mom our usual see you soon kiss. Off I went into the freezing, sterile room wearing my annoying hair cap thing, booties, and an over-sized hospital gown. I didn't care about the gown so much, I knew it would be only a short period of time until it would be taken off anyway. They had me move over to the operating table and bundled me up with some warm blankets. The nurses were very nice and they were very good at comforting me. They put these leg things on me that felt like someone was massaging my legs but it was to keep the blood flow going. We didn't want any blood clots forming, been there, done that. My arm that had the IV in it was put straight out next to me. Since it was so cold in there and my arm was the only exposed part of my body it actually felt good. Like when you're in bed and you're getting hot and then you move your leg or arm to a new spot under the covers and it's nice and cool. There were a lot of people in the room setting things up and doing their jobs like they would any other day. Little did we know what was the last time I'd feel normal and fully functional and independent for a very long time. Let the loss of control begin.

5 WAKING UP

After what I had just gone through all I could think about was Manu? Who was going to feed him? Did they know what times to feed him and how much? How would he get taken outside to go to the bathroom? Did they know to change his pee pads and where to find new ones? Did they know how to give him his medicine? And did they know how to put on his confusing harness he had to wear so that when he bolted he didn't snap his neck? Worrying that my overweight chihuahua would miss me and now I was stuck in this hospital for who knows how long. Mom decided to stay with me and Dad was supposed to be leaving the country for a work related trip to France. It's moments like this that I regret being a pet owner. I must have been in shock. This is what came to mind when I woke up from my surgery unable to move?! Forget the fact that we didn't know what exactly happened and how/if this was going to be fixable. I wasn't thinking of my job or paying my bills or if I'd ever be able to walk again. My body was being pumped with drugs, I couldn't press the nurse button, I was in excruciating pain and all I could think about was the damn dog. He wasn't even technically mine. My older sister, Mick, adopted him when she was living in Queens. She ended up moving to Italy with my younger sister, Rose, and left him with me. He wouldn't have survived traveling to another country. He had seizures. Every night he had to be given his potassium bromide. The easiest way to get him to take his medicine was to squirt it over some nasty and expensive wet dog food. It worked like a charm, at least better than when I tried putting a piece of hot dog on the end of the medicine squirter thing and then when he'd bite the piece I'd shoot the medicine into his mouth. This was a reoccurring theme for the next couple of months, I was faced with some difficult circumstances and yet I was constantly worrying about and missing my dog. I would think of ways to sneak him into the building and hide him in my room. He was tiny so he could easily fit into a purse. He is deaf so all the strange noises around wouldn't bother him. But he was a jealous dog so if someone was trying to help me he most likely would attack them.

The first eight days after surgery I was penned up in Baltimore at the hospital. I spent some time in the Intensive-Care Unit right after my operation. They had to monitor me closely because I was having a horrible reaction to some steroids that were given to me there. All I remember from that whole ordeal was hearing my heart monitor thing beeping way too fast and not feeling so great. I was trying to figure out what was happening and was looking around frantically at everyone around me. My mom was there. I could hear her yelling at the staff. She was demanding to know what they were doing and why they were not doing anything. I was in and out of my drug induced sleep, thank God. I might have been in shock, and that was helpful for my mental stability. I wasn't able to tell what was really going on or understand the outcome of the surgery and still did not know that I had extensive nerve damage. I couldn't talk because of the tube down my throat. I recall only a few short details from those few hours in there, one of which was not wanting to see or talk to anyone. That feeling of wanting to be left alone would last for quite some time to come. I didn't want people telling me everything would be okay and that I was strong and would get through this. I needed to come to that realization on my own.

As I was being moved from the ICU to a regular one-patient room (which I did have to pay extra for out of my own pocket- a whole $25) I thought I was in a bad dream. They had these goons rolling me down the hallways and they seemed to not have taken the maneuvering a large hospital bed class. I thought they were joking around or something. I didn't appreciate them laughing at my expense, but there was no laughing involved, which made it even worse, they really did not know what they were doing. We went what seemed like the longest and shadiest way possible. The elevator was so old and dirty it felt like we were taking it because the regular one was broken down or something so this was the last resort. It might have been one of those under-construction elevators where they put up the quilted pads to protect the walls and leave a cut-out for the buttons. Or a food service elevator where the stink of the food stays inside the shaft for eternity only to be covered up with a new disgusting smell with the next meal. Well, as we were getting onto one of the disgusting elevators they crashed me into the side and couldn't maneuver me in the right way so that I fit through the doors and they closed on me. Yeah, add getting squashed while attempting to get on an elevator to the list of crazy things happening to me that day. They were trying to get me off of the elevator and through the doors they knocked me around a bit more and I felt my IV shift. I said something to them and they looked at my arm and told me that nothing happened. I asked the nurse once we got settled into my room and it was not just an odd feeling I had, they ripped both of my IVs out. They had to put all new ones into my arm. Thanks a lot. I just wanted to sleep and get comfortable. My back and legs were still numb from the epidural so I knew in the back of my head it was only going to become more painful in the next few hours. The room was spacious until they had to bring in the fold-up bed for my mom to sleep in. There was a large recliner chair and a window the length of one of the walls. Fittingly, the sky was grey and dreary out. I wasn't the only one having a crappy day.

My nights were spent sleepless. Trying to think of anything but the pain. Calling out my mom's name so that she could call in a nurse to help shift my position in bed or give me more pain medicine. Waiting as long as possible between requests so that I wouldn't aggravate my mom or the staff since I was making so many of them. It would come and go in waves, although it seemed that the worst and longest lasting part was anything that involved the sharp pains in my lower back or pressure on the back of my head. As soon as I was turned to one side to relieve the other I felt like the discomfort would shift to something different. It was a constant struggle of trying to keep my mind in a better place and staying in the moment.

Right when I thought I was seeing the light at the end of the tunnel, it would suddenly disappear. I would be making strides and showing some progress and then the rug would be pulled right out from under me. It was hard for me to see that I was making progress in the first place. I was the one inside this screwed up body and felt like nothing was getting better. It was important to have those people around me who recognized when my body was doing something different and improved. First was the devastation of being aware of the fact that surgery was over and it didn't go as planned and I really wasn't able to move and it wasn't just going to go away overnight or the next few days. That journey of trying to get back to my norm was just beginning and I had no clue how long it would take. At first I was so highly medicated that I think it didn't truly sink in that I wasn't moving my body and was quite cognizant of that, but then the surgical team that was under my orthopedic doctor would come into the hospital room every day and ask the same questions and test the same areas for some sort of response. It was frustrating for me because it was a constant confirmation that something had gone terribly wrong. It was a bad dream and I wanted to wake up. The team would come in and ask me to move this finger and that foot and squeeze their hand. I would try and my brain was telling that body part to do what they were asking and then they'd repeat their request and that is when I knew there was a total disconnect with my brain and body. I told them I WAS doing what they were saying. I wanted to move my finger. I wanted to wiggle my toes and lift my leg, so much so that I wanted to kick them in the face. It was as if they didn't believe that I was trying. They would repeat their request to move this or that and I had to tell them calmly that I was trying and that I was not some person being lazy or not trying my hardest. It felt like they were accusing me of being a sub-par patient. They obviously did not know me or listen to what I was telling them. If I was challenged I would step up to it (figuratively speaking) and give more than my all. That team of doctors really bothered me, but I think they angered my mom even more. She wanted to ream them out and tell them to get lost and that they didn't know how to do their jobs. She would ask them questions they didn't know how to answer. Or ask for solutions and explanations they would not know how to give. They were chasing their tails in circles. The whole situation seemed like something foreign to them and they were scrambling to avoid the hard answers and questions. We wanted to know what happened, when we would see the doctor, if this was permanent, how long we'd have to stay in that shit hole of a hospital and where we would go next, what did we have to do to get me better, why the staff was so unprepared and brainless, why wasn't my pain team doing their job to manage my pain, why weren't they checking my neck wound as often and my back? It felt all we were doing was asking questions and all they were doing was avoiding answers.

After the whirl wind of finding out I couldn't control my body we started to focus on the problems that were brought about. One of them would be my neck and the brace they didn't fit properly. I was having extreme pain where the brace was rubbing on the back of my head, under my jaw, and on my collarbones. I thought it was just a new pain that I had to deal with and try to manage by shifting positions frequently so that the pressure would be lessened there. I thought it was okay that the nurses were not turning me and not taking my brace off to look at everything. I didn't say anything about that because honestly I did not feel comfortable with them to remove my brace safely. They did not give me the reasons to have confidence in them. I thought if they attempted something like that that my head would fall off or my fusion would break apart. Now I know that I was overreacting, but at the time I felt like I was being totally reasonable with those fears. My mom finally got sick of waiting for them to do their job and asked why they weren't checking my neck and of course they had no answer. They mumbled out some excuses and went to go "look at my chart" which was code for figure out what the hell they were going to do. The nurse came back in after a good fifteen minutes with supplies in hand. She asked mom to help, imagine that, a nurse too afraid to proceed on her own. With my mom assisting I felt better, but I am sure the nurse still felt like she was breathing down her neck. They turned me to one side and removed half the brace and decided to do it one side at a time. It was absolutely disgusting. It had been a few days (when it should have been more like a few times PER day) since my surgery and they cleaned up the newly healing scar and all the clotted blood stuck throughout my hair. The area around the incision was all shaved free of my hair and was already starting to become itchy growing back in. The worst part for me was the nasty stench that was coming from back there- the crease of the back of my head and neck was rotting. Yeah, nasty, a crease full of dead raunchy skin. They took quite a long time just to clean that up with q-tips and alcohol. All I cared about was how good it felt to have that brace off. Next on the agenda was the two gaping gashes in my head from the back of the brace digging in. It was so bad that it was still bleeding for days to come. They had to clean that up and put some gauze on it to try to get it to scab over. We also put some new padding on my brace because the one I had been wearing was soaked in blood and skin. Ew. My mom was super upset about the two holes from my brace and rightly so. I couldn't see them so I am sure they looked worse than they felt. To me it was just a literal headache. Turns out after all my hair grew back those two spots remain bald and look as if they will remain that way forever because now there is scar tissue where those spots were and I know from experience that hair does not grow where there is a scar. My mom made sure to have them check and clean my brace more often.

I had never even heard of a rehab hospital except in the context of addictive behaviors. The social worker came by my hospital room to discuss discharge and what we were going to do after we were done there. We had no idea. I needed special care that my mom could not provide for me. We weren't prepared or informed of what to do in a situation like this. That is when she came in with the rehab idea. My surgeon actually told my mom that it wasn't necessary, but she had no clue how she was going to care for me or get me better. There was a rehabilitation hospital only twenty minutes from my house that the social worker had researched and it turned out they accepted my insurance and had a room available there for me. When I was discharged from the hospital that is where I would go. I was told they would provide transportation for me since I still was unable to move and function independently. It would be like having my own limo, only it was a ambulance-bus thing and they weren't taking me to a fun event.

6 REHAB

The first impression of the rehab hospital was a good one, but, I was high on drugs from the transport, so what did I know? Two medics came to get me from the hospital bed in the early afternoon. I felt like a free woman- all the I.V.s and other contraptions that were hooked up to me were taken off that morning. I was now on to taking pills orally and peeing in a bed pan. They strapped me, with at least 4 straps, to the gurney. It was very skinny. I don't know how a regular size person fits on those things. My nurse gave me an extra dosage of valium. Once I was loaded in to the transport ambulance I remember maybe 10 minutes of the 2 hour ride. As they rolled me into my new residence it seemed like a nice, big place. Little did I know that this is what I'd call home for the next seven weeks. My room seemed comfortable- big bed, flat screen television, plenty of nurses, and a recliner for visitors. One of the best parts was that I had a nice big window that I could let real sunlight come through. Unfortunately it was the kind that didn't open so I wasn't able to enjoy fresh air. Oh well, at least I had my window.

It made me think of my cubicle at work that didn't have a window anywhere near it...I would kill for a window in my office. The supply closet had a window, why couldn't I have one!?

After I was moved in to my new bed and ready to continue sleeping, my mom went home to eat dinner. I made her promise to come right back. I was nervous to be without her in a place like that. I didn't feel confident with the staff. My feelings were spot on. I asked the nurse for my next dosage of medications and she gave me less than what I normally took. I questioned this and she said it was according to the doctor's orders. I hadn't even seen the doctor there yet; how could they already be changing things like that? It made me super mad because it took us days to regulate my pain. I took what she gave me and just hoped it would be enough. My anxiety was starting to rise. It only got worse. A woman walked in telling me she was the physical therapist and was there to get me out of bed, into my wheelchair, and off to dinner in the cafeteria. There were so many things wrong with this, it was ridiculous. First, I told her I hadn't been able to sit up and that we haven't even attempted to sit me up at a normal angle. She didn't seem to listen. Then, I told her I hadn't sat in a wheelchair and didn't see how she was going to get me in one by herself. Lastly, I didn't understand why I was going to the cafeteria because not only was I not hungry but I also couldn't move to feed myself. She still paid me no mind. She came in and just picked me up. I started to go a bit crazy. I think it was a mixture of my anxiety and lack of pain meds. I started to literally cry out in pain. She panicked. That didn't make things any better. Instead of putting me in the wheelchair she decided to just stick me in the recliner. It was too big to give me any constructive support. I scared her off. The nurse came in and I got her to get me a phone and call home. I told mom I needed her there right away between my sobs. I wasn't even able to explain to her what happened. She arrived in 20 minutes.

After that ordeal I settled in. They had a white board next to my bed (which was very annoying because I couldn't turn my head to see it) that the nurses and aides wrote on. They would write who was on for that shift/day and what time I had physical therapy and occupational therapy. One useful thing they listed was the date; all the days seemed to bleed together. I saw the aides more than the nurses. They came around every few hours to check my vitals and see if I needed anything. I liked them the most. Especially the 3-10 shift; they were fun and young. It was nice to have someone near my age in there since all the patients were old farts. They didn't make me do things I didn't want to do. They never forced me to go to the cafeteria. Once I started using the port-a-pot they wanted to have me use it constantly, but I got out of it without a fight during the evening. I played on their fears of not knowing how to help me or move me. It also helped that there weren't as many people on staff during the night which made it harder for them to get the job done let alone a thorough job.

I had two therapists- one for occupational therapy and one for physical therapy. I got my first OT in trouble. He ended up giving his notice about 2 weeks later anyway so I didn't have to worry about him. At first I liked him and he wasn't too bad to look at, but that wore off quickly. His confidence turned to vanity and I noticed more and more his man boobs and slight beer gut. He had horrible taste in clothing as well. One time he was wearing a virtual belly shirt. The love handles wanted to be seen by all I guess. His nice hair turned to very greasy or over gelled. It was like when you'd go to camp when you're younger and find this boy who you think is so amazing and you are shocked to find out he likes you back (after receiving a note passed from his best friend to yours asking if you liked him, check yes or no) and you hang out and think you're in love with him. But the real world comes along and after camp he no longer returns your calls or emails. He starts to become unattractive to you and you start drawing on his face or poking his eyeballs out in all the photographs. You even cut him completely out of some of the pictures and put them back up on your cork board sans camp boy. You finally are over it and move on, but sadly will make that mistake over and over. It's part of growing up. It's not funny at that time, but now you can hear a song that brings you back to those days and chuckle to yourself, it isn't so bad. Don't get me wrong, I wouldn't want to re-live those days, but going through it once wasn't as hellish as I thought at the time. Now if I could only apply that thinking to therapy and get myself through that.

Within the first few days of therapy I thought he did something to my shoulder. He was trying to make me lift and push weight up towards the ceiling to strengthen my arm muscles. I did a few reps and then felt my shoulder crack and pop. The first one didn't hurt, but after it happening over and over it started to get progressively worse. I told him what I was feeling in my shoulder and that it was painful and he said that I didn't know what real pain was and to keep going. I did the best I could but it was not a good way to start off with therapy. I mentioned this incident to my mom who got heated about it and complained to someone in charge. They had to order an x-ray, it was that bad. I was told that I could change therapists if I wanted to. Of course I wanted to. I opted for a new therapist and ended up getting the one in charge. She was in her late twenties and had only been there for a year or so. She was the one to have. She put me to work and challenged me but not to the point of going over board. She spiced things up and came up with ideas outside of the box; some were lame, but others were very motivating. Her habit of talking to patients like we were nuts or children could get old, but I don't think it was insincere. She genuinely wanted to help improve your situation and knew the little things counted. Her recognition of that and the way she emoted her praise could make you feel like she was dealing with an invalid, but then I had to remember, we were invalids. We were all on drugs and in shock from whatever happened to us, so it was right of her to act basically and simply. She was put together and on top of everything, which are characteristics I tend to gravitate towards in a normal situation, but being the one she was trying to fix didn't make me like her any more. She would group a few of us together to play against each other in Wii bowling or tennis. Some of them would stand to play and work on their balance and some of us would sit and try to just move our arm fast enough so that the ball would move. I stunk at the bowling game, I seemed to drop the ball a lot right at my side or throw it so slowly it would get stuck in the middle of the lane. Some guys would be competitive, but not with other people; they would challenge themselves and get all worked up over it if they weren't doing well. That's when they would need a break. I had to work with putty and I hated this exercise. I would have to roll it into a log or snake and pinch it with each finger over and over, and I would get so frustrated by the time I reached the pinky and it would make no indent. Another "game" she had me work on was with the putty and these tiny, plastic peg-like things. She would have me pick each peg up individually and put it into the putty. Then I had to roll it all around and get all the pegs covered and hidden. After that, I had to go through the wad of putty and pull out each peg, digging and pushing and pulling. This was all work for my left hand. I still couldn't hold a cup or utensil, she was working to help me get my motor skills going. Meanwhile, my right arm would just hang out, resting on my lap or on the table. It started getting gross when we were working with velcro and ripping pieces off a board covered in velcro or having to turn a block that was stuck to it. I wasn't using my hands that much and wasn't washing them so the skin was starting to peel as if I had had a sunburn. And all my dead skin would flake off on the velcro exercise and turn it from black to white. Nasty dead skin. I said something to my OT and she just waved it away like it was no big deal. I was just hoping they would clean it after I was done using it. Otherwise, that would mean that they didn't clean any of the props they had patients use for exercise and that meant other people's dead skin and other nasty bodily fluids or even solids were all over them. That got me thinking and I started noticing these types of things. Like the guy across the way exercising by picking his nose or the wrinkly lady with white hair that coughed constantly as if she was hacking up a hairball and never covered her mouth. But they did handle some situations well: a stroke patient sitting next to me at the hand therapy table couldn't communicate and ended up urinating on himself. It was noticed by one of the aides because it was dripping from his wheelchair into a puddle on the floor. They took care of it discreetly and respectfully which was very kind and professional of them. I don't even think anyone spoke, they just took care of it and moved on as if nothing happened. It was odd to see them being so discreet. Especially because the day before, I overheard some strange conversations going on in the gym about last poops or how this patient was refusing therapy and that they were fine with it because she smelled like urine. Totally ignoring that whole patient confidentiality clause. It made me wonder what types of things they would say about me. Maybe they would tell each other to check out my super long, dark leg hair. Or the fact that I hadn't shaved my stinky armpits since my surgery. The greasy hair that we just brushed back every morning was the most obvious potential coffee talk. But the most embarrassing for me was the fact that I had to wear diapers; I wouldn't want to know what they would say about that.

I usually had OT in the afternoons right after lunch so I would be sleepy. And some of those exercises made me want to pull my hair out. I had a one pound pink weight to do about 10 different exercises. I think they made me do those because it took so long and it gave my therapist the opportunity to go and work with one of her other gazillion patients she had all at once. To say they were understaffed is an understatement. I remember one day my coffee's caffeine just wasn't kicking in for me and I my eyelids felt like they were so swollen and droopy. I was given my weight and instructions on what to do with it and off she went to pay attention to a different person. I finished my exercises. She was still busy with someone else. I improvised and did some of my own body building. That didn't last too long; there are only so many things you can do with a tiny weight and gimpy arms. I decided to just sit there and relax and take a break from it. I caught myself nodding off. It felt like my head was falling and crashing down, but in reality it barely moved. My cheeks and ears went red immediately, but as I looked around, nobody was even paying attention and what made it even funnier was that I saw so many of the old people around falling asleep too!

Towards the end of my stay at rehab the OT put together a therapy idea that was great for almost all the ladies but me- manicures. I couldn't even lift my own right arm up to the table; my left hand had to assist, and once my right arm was actually up and on the table it would slide and flop right off. It would only stay if my left hand was keeping it there and how would I paint my nails if that hand had to be held in position? Plus, I was not going to be able to have my left hand painted because how would my right hand even hold the nail polish brush? Instead, I felt tortured because I just sat there and watched everyone else have fun and get their nails all painted up pretty. When the activity was almost over one of the therapists realized that my nails weren't done. I had to explain myself because they just thought I was being ornery and not wanting to participate. I had to show them that my hand would just fall off the table and I wasn't able to grasp the brush to swipe my nails. They let me off the hook, but they didn't really have an option or better idea. Whatever, my mom made me feel better later that day and gave me a nice pedicure in the sun outside on the black, hot, metal bench by the entrance of the rehab building. I soaked up the sun. It was just what I needed to lift my spirits that afternoon.

One of my first tasks was to learn to stay sitting up. I had lost all control of the muscles to keep my upper body up. I could only sit with a support and even that was work and tired me out. This scared me. I couldn't wrap my mind around the fact that I couldn't even sit up on my own. Was this just a horrible dream from eating some weird food earlier in the day? When was I going to wake up from it and go back to normal? After my therapist had worked me up to being able to sit on my own for more than five minutes I started to accept where I was and what was happening. It was no use to just simmer in my "could have, would have, should haves". I learned I needed all my energy to concentrate on the task at hand, whether it be sitting up or tapping my feet or doing butt squeezes. All of these little exercises were building me back up to where I was before. Whenever I started to get too comfortable with one exercise they would bump my regiment up to the next level. One day my physical therapist wanted me to do some exercises laying down and she went to move me and lay me down when I felt my back crack. I freaked out. My thoughts were going wild in my head. I was so scared that something had happened to my spine and the rod they had just screwed into it. It made me feel sick and she must have seen my face turn white like a ghost because she asked me if I was alright. I told her I felt my back crack and asked if that meant that I shouldn't move. She reassured me it was just the vertebrae in my back adjusting and it was nothing bad and it didn't indicate a problem.

A few weeks into physical therapy I thought I was going to have a heart attack. I was starting to feel comfortable with sitting up unassisted. And by unassisted I mean for no more than five minutes at a time and someone sitting right next to me watching and waiting for me to fall. My therapist had me do some warm up exercises like my butt squeezes and leg lifts, but she wasn't being to hard on me like usual. I began to notice she was bringing different props over to where I was sitting. She brought out a small walker with an arm support on the right side. That was the moment I felt myself beginning to sweat and my heart beat started to go faster. I honestly didn't think I was ready enough to stand, with or without support. She began to explain to me how we were going to do this. I could feel the blood draining from my face. She could see the anxiety in my eyes and tried to reassure me that I could do it and she was going to have two others help her. I had one person in the front of me holding the walker steady and then one person on each side of me to help me up and hold me up. I didn't want to think about it anymore, I just wanted to get it over with.

Sharp pain was surging through my legs. My knees felt like they were glass and on the verge of breaking into a million little pieces. I didn't think my ankles were going to be able to hold my weight. When they lifted me up to stand they put my right, gimpy arm into the holder and guided my left arm up and onto the walker's handle. My wrist bent into an unnatural-looking position and my elbow began aching. I wanted to sit back down the moment they lifted my butt off the mat. I thought the incision on my back was going to bust open and my head was going to fall off my neck.

I went along and did what she wanted so that I could sit back down. I wasn't thinking that it was going to be a process of repeating this over and over and challenging my body to learn how to stand and then walk again. The plan of it all was far from my mind. I could barely handle the present, let alone what was in store for me the next time I had therapy or a few days from that moment. The only thing I was able to do was repeat, "I can do all things through Christ who strengthens me" over and over in my head.

The things they made us do were so infantile at times. Throwing bean bags into a hoop really made me mad, so I just took it out on it. I would have to extend my limp and heavy arm to where ever they held out the bean bag square and I'd have to grab a hold of it and then toss it into the goal. This was so frustrating at first because I could barely reach the bean bag and then to keep it in my grasp required so much concentration and exertion I would be sweating just from that. The worst of it all was chucking the bag. I couldn't get my brain and arm and hand to work together. In my head I would just think okay, release your grip and toss the bag, but my hand would respond.

Emotions run high in this place, especially in the gym. You can feel the heaviness of it all there. It isn't just the patients that contribute to it either. The families come around and watch like hawks to make sure all is done according to their own standards, the nurses run around frantically trying to accomplish their checklist and the therapists shuffle from one to the next giving exercises to do until they return.

The gym is a complete fake. The first time I was whisked by the entrance I thought it was so amazing and had such up-to-date facilities. I couldn't have been more wrong. It was one gigantic room with a 2 story-high ceiling and a lot of windows. That was the part that I liked. It gave it a feeling of space and airiness. With all the old sick people doing their therapy it needed to be well ventilated. There were table mats lined up across one wall, an area that had private mats with curtains, a few pieces of exercise equipment on the far wall, a room with the exercise pool, an exit to an outdoor patio with a few ramps for a change in scenery, and the staff station beyond that. It was usually blocked and backed up with a bunch of people in wheelchairs who were finished with their therapy session and waiting for someone to push them back to their room or to the cafeteria.

What bothered me most was the pool and the patio. In the 7 weeks I was there, twice a day, I did not see one person using those therapeutic options. In my head this was ridiculous. Those two things are not only fun, but great ways of healing oneself. I wanted to go outside so badly to do my exercises and breathe fresh air; I would have done anything to escape the 4 walls I was constantly trapped in. The weather was beautiful for May and June, but it was not convenient for the therapists to have their patients out there. They wouldn't even just prop the doors open when it would have been a perfect way to get some stagnant air and bad energy out. The pool was such a teaser. As someone with arthritis and bad joints the water is the ideal way for building my muscles and staying strong because it's less stressful on my body. I am able to do an hour workout without any difficulties in the pool and if I was doing that routine on land I wouldn't even be able to last 5 minutes. This had been my method of therapy and exercise for the past few years. My surgeon had requested that I used that after my wounds were healed but the rehab hospital refused. There weren't enough therapists to go around, so they couldn't spare one to be working only with me in the pool and they didn't have a lifeguard. These were the lame excuses we had to deal with. We asked several times to go in the pool to try and change their minds but they didn't budge.

So I was restricted to the mats and tables with the other 20 or so invalids.

Another thing that everyone had to share was the therapy dogs. Every week 2 or 3 certified therapy golden retrievers were brought into the gym to work with patients. They would help people walk distances, they'd retrieve balls that were thrown for arm exercise, or even would sit next to you so that you could pat them. At first I thought this was a brilliant thing and I became very excited to work with them. It looked like a great way to brighten my day. They seemed to be very calming and joyful. Unfortunately, these dogs ended up annoying me when I saw them coming in to help. My first experience with them was the cause of such bitterness. The therapist asked if I wanted to spend some time working with the dog, and of course I said yes. I missed my dog and wasn't able to see him so I thought this could work as a substitution and I'd be working out. The dogs came and the owner had one of them sit next to my wheelchair. I could barely lift my arm and hand to pet his head. It was impossible to do anything with the dog at that point in time. So instead, I had to sit there and watch everyone else enjoy the dog and work with him. I felt teased and defeated. I couldn't even pet him! After my surgery there were a lot of things that were piling up that I could no longer do. Just add that to the list. It was so frustrating to me to think that only a few weeks earlier I was doing so much and going somewhere with my life and then it was halted to a major stop and I found myself laying in a hospital bed unable to move. I needed to change that thought process of all the things I couldn't do to all the things I would be doing eventually. I had to take it moment by moment.

Deb, oh Deb. My first encounter with Deb wasn't actually seeing her. I had been hearing some extremely strange moaning. It sounded like someone was dying. It had an ambulance siren effect; she would start in her room and as they rolled her down the hallway it would get louder and louder as she approached my doorway, then it would quiet down once she was all the way at the other end of the wing. I didn't know what to make of it. I noticed it was occurring more frequently. I decided to ask the nurse what that noise was and she just rolled her eyes and said, Deb. Then I saw her one day in therapy across the way. I recognized her by the bellowing. It actually would turn into yelling or arguing. She was tall and skinny and very unsteady. Her IV pole was always connected to her. She would wear old baggie t-shirts with rock bands from the eighties on them. Her fingernails were very long and I wondered if she wanted them like that or if no one offered to cut them. She had a monotone voice and would constantly request to go back to her room. It turns out she had a brain aneurism. She had a stroke and it caused her to lose almost all of her ability to move her legs and right arm. I am not sure, but she seemed to have some mental challenges from that incident as well. It wasn't her first time in rehab either, so the staff seemed mostly annoyed with her and her act. Was she just acting out and being disruptive on purpose, or was that her only way of knowing how to communicate that something was not right? Well, one day I was being wheeled across the gym to do occupational therapy with another patient. I could hear who it was before I even saw her, Deb. She was doing her usual complaining bit, trying to get out of whatever exercise she was working on. I pulled up to the table and we sat there together. I didn't know what to say or if I should even say anything so I ended up smiling.

Deb decided to speak first, and instead of the usual, "Hi how are you?" she just blurted out, "How old are you?". I told her twenty-four and she then said, "Oh, I thought you were twelve or something.". Whatever, not the first time in my life that someone has gotten my age confused. For some reason, I just pointed to my chest and asked her, "How many twelve year olds do you know that have these?". My therapist died laughing and so did Deb, a good start with a humorous note that involved my boobs. From that moment on, Deb decided we were going to be buddies. Anytime she would go by my room she would shout out a, "Hey Ang!" to me. Or if we were in the gym together (which would be most afternoons) she would watch me do my therapy and root me on. She really was an encourager and lightened the mood. It made it less painful to stand or walk when Deb was right there telling me to keep going and that I was doing a great job. In the cafeteria if we were both in there she would try and sit with me, and if she was there first and had a space open I would have the nurse put me next to her. I was always curious to know what would come out of her mouth next. She could get me laughing, that is for sure. One day I was eating outside on the patio by myself and she came outside with some guests; her mom and dad were visiting. They joined me at my table and we had a great lunch together. Some people found Deb extremely annoying and difficult to deal with, but I thought she was a riot and had a very caring heart. That deserves some respect and sometimes they didn't give her that. It is hard to put yourself in someone else's shoes, especially if you have to care for that person and they wear you down, but it is so important to go above and beyond and really understand what they are going through and have some compassion.

Every morning mom would arrive around 8am and get me ready for the day. For her to even do that was time consuming. She had to get up early to get herself ready and take care of the dog and cats and then drive 20 minutes (if there was no traffic) to the rehab. Once she got there she would help me finish up whatever I was eating for breakfast. I tried to order something she would like to eat because I knew she would not have taken the time to grab a bite to eat before she left the house. We had a routine by the end of it all; we'd have breakfast and watch the news (even though it was the most annoying reports/hosts). Then she would get me all washed up. This is where the good smelling soaps and lotions would come in- about the only thing in that room, including myself, that was safe to smell. She would fill up the ugly pink plastic basin with warm soapy water and wash each part of me. She would do it in shifts- wash a body part and then dry it- so that I wouldn't get cold. We would purposefully get the sheets wet so that the aides would have to change them. Next up was lotion time. It was very therapeutic for my nerve regrowth whenever she would rub my arms or legs. It seemed to stimulate them. I would have to pick out some sweats and a shirt with a massive hole cut around the neck so that it would fit over my neck-brace with ease. Early on we discovered that the shirts were going to be an issue so mom went out and bought a number of cheap t-shirts from a craft store that are meant to have iron-on decals and things of that nature. She found some fun colors, to brighten me up a bit however we could. She took the scissors to the shirt's collar and voila- easy and comfortable fitting t-shirt that was big enough to make me feel OK not to wear a bra or need a sweater over it. Score! After I was dressed and ready to go with my bright colored hospital grippy socks, she would help the nurses get me into my wheelchair. It took three people to do that. This was a very scary thing for me. They would make the bed flat and use a small square piece of fabric called a chucks to swivel me 90 degrees and then slid me to the edge of the bed. It took one person on each side of me up by my head/arms and then someone down at my legs so they could all lift at the same time and scooch me into the chair. I was so nervous that one of them would lift higher or lower then the other and then I'd just roll out of their arms onto the floor or that they would shift me the wrong way and hurt my back or neck. Many times only minor things would happen; for example, since I could not move my arm on my own it would often just drop to the side of my body when they lifted me or I would sit on it once they moved me or my legs would just drop and bang into things. I survived. It was a daily occurrence that I dreaded and would give anything to get out of but it was so necessary for my recovery. After the move we'd get my teeth all brushed up, using a barf pan to rinse. Thank goodness for the electrical toothbrush that did all the hard work for me, I just had to move it around in my mouth. Just in case it didn't do the job I would always make sure to pop a piece of gum into my mouth so I wouldn't kill my therapists and nurses with my dragon breath. We even had a special compartment for the gum storage- in the lap table that would roll over the bed there was a hidden drawer big enough for a few packs of gum.

The therapy aid was always waiting for me at the door to finish up and would whisk me away to the gym for my daily dose of torture. I would get a kiss from my mom and a see-you-later-tonight. Yes, every night she would come back. And that would be after working all day long at her shop or running errands or doing other things that never got enough of her time because I seemed to be consuming it all. Most of the time she would bring a meal from home for me to eat or save for later. I ended up having a shelf to myself with all the goodies labeled Piazza in the patient fridge they had for us. My mom would stay all evening, get me ready for bed, then go home. She would sit in the recliner chair that was in the corner of my room and we'd watch television together. I wasn't up for another transfer out of my bed into my chair at night so we just stayed put. It was an exciting time. And I would usually nod off, so it's not even like I was that great of company. But she still showed up every morning and every night. I would have been in much worse shape mentally and emotionally if she had done otherwise. She spent over sixty-five hours alone driving back and forth those seven weeks. My dad would come at night when he could and would bring me ice-cream with sprinkles. I don't know why, but I was on a sprinkle kick. I even had my own stash of sprinkles in my closet. My aunt and uncle would come a few nights of the week too. It was nice to have all that company. We didn't even have to do anything special, just sit there and hang out together and watch television and relax. My aunt would come in a few days of the week too. She worked from home so she was able to get away for lunch or take her computer with her and do work in my room just so that I would have company.

The brace had to stay on my neck for 6 months. I went through four braces in that time. They tried to customize them as much as possible. The first two were horrible. I developed two raw holes on the back of my head that eventually scarred over and turned into bald spots. I had contusions on my collar bones from where the bottom of my brace would rub and dig into. My ears had begun to really bother me and the pain wouldn't go away. I told my doctor over and over and finally they realized it wasn't my ear that was the problem but that my brace was putting extreme pressure on my jaw and therefore caused TMJ: the nerves were being restricted. The feeling of throbbing and sharp shooting pain near my ear could not be treated. It was the worst at night and then when I woke up in the morning. We started to put heat on my face in the morning to reduce the pain. After I got home I found a different supplier and they brought me a new brace and customized it to me at my house. My symptoms of TMJ went away after a few days. That guy knew what he was doing, cutting away and reshaping the plastic pieces of the brace. It was so difficult to find the right brace because my neck is so short but my head is so big. I was in-between two different types and sizes of the neck brace. So he improvised and made it work. That one lasted the longest. We changed the pads frequently and the plastic shape seemed to hold out longer and it felt like my head was being more supported and less strained. There still was the problem of adjusting it every morning. It never felt straight on. Any time we took it off or tightened it I had to readjust to it because it would feel totally crooked. When I showered we had a different brace we put on; it had less material (and a lot less support) which made it easier to get to everything to wash. It felt like heaven when we took that thing off. I also felt naked without it. It's like when you always wear a watch and then one day you forget to wear it and it just throws you off.

It was a constant battle between relieving the pressure on my jaw and chin or on my collar bones. When I would lay down flat there would be less weight on my jaw, but there was still the problem of the front of the brace digging into my skin. My mom would try to manipulate the plastic of the brace so that it wouldn't cause abrasions. It was cut and bent and padded. At first that provided relief, but that was only temporary and it always came back until we did something different. The problem with doing all of that is that it would alter the brace and cause the structural integrity to be lost. I was so paranoid about my neck moving and thus ruining the fusion so I thought I better not have it messed around with too much and just deal with it.

There was a closet in my room. It was your typical two sided closet with shelves on one side and a hanging rod on the other. It was where we stashed very important things. They wouldn't do laundry quickly enough sometimes, so we hoarded towels and facecloths. My mom would go in the linen closet and if they were there then she'd take extras to keep in the room for emergencies. That was a good thing too; there were many times of emergency. By the end of my stay she noticed the staff had put up a letter on the linen closet warning patients and caregivers not to take extras. This is a prime example of one of those rules made to be broken. We also stockpiled briefs. No, not men's underwear, but diapers. We had to get the petite size from the supply closet. The nurses could never find the right size when they went to look for me, so my mom would check now and again and grab some. The normal items that go in a closet were kept there too- socks, sweatpants, sweatshorts, t-shirts with the necks cut off so it could fit over my neck-brace, and lots of oversized undies.

My closet also housed my tons of candy. Why is it that when someone is sick that everyone sends candy? I didn't mind. I couldn't eat most of it so it kept my visitors very happy. I had become obsessed with french burnt peanuts- the ones that are coated in that red, bumpy hard shell. The variety was great and I never ran low. One of my friends from work went to the local market and bought baggies upon baggies of assorted penny candy. Another friend who lived in NYC ordered a gift package from Hershey Chocolate World and had it sent to me. It was the most chocolate I've ever owned at once in my entire life. There was a giant candy bar that had the words "Get Well Spangie" iced on it, a tin of kisses, a box of chocolate cordials, and a huge box of the different brands of bite size chocolate bars they make. I had a thirst for peach tea so we kept a case of that in the bottom. On the outside of the closet my mom would tape up all the cards people sent me. It was a good visual reminder that people really were thinking of me and wishing me well and keeping me in their prayers. It was my wall of encouragement. We (and by we I mean my mom) had to rearrange them a couple of times because it had gotten so crowded. The mail lady knew my room number without even looking after the first week. I guess most patients only stay up to a maximum of 1-2 weeks so they didn't have mail coming through as much. Sometimes I'd get the same exact card from a few different people; that always cracked me up. Of all the get well cards out there and they happen to choose the same one. I loved having that closet...it was a treasure chest for me. My stockpile of all the things I could want at the time. That thing took a very long time to pack up.

Next to the closet was a sink and an area where we put all my toiletries. There also was a huge bathroom in my room which I didn't use as a real bathroom until the last week I was there. Instead, it became the parking garage/medical equipment storage area. Whenever I wasn't in my wheelchair we parked it in the bathroom so there would be more room. My walker and port-a-pot stayed in there too. If we ended up having some guests we didn't have to worry about where they would sit, just pull one of the extra chairs out from the bathroom! It was very convenient. The thing I hated most about that bathroom was the shower. It was just a huge space with a drain in the floor, safety bars on all walls for grabbing, and a removable showerhead. It was the worst thing I had to do in rehab. I was happy to be clean in the end, but it was so shadowed by the process of what had to be done to get to that point that made me very resistant to showers. I stuck with my sponge baths for over six weeks.

The cafeteria had one of those freezers with all different types of ice creams like the ice-cream sandwich or nutty buddy or the little cups of chocolate and vanilla ice-cream in one. My ultimate favorite was the moose tracks ice-cream cone. I would always check to see if they had any, but I guess I wasn't the only one who really liked that one. Vanilla ice-cream with swirls of chocolate and peanut butter and little chocolate covered pieces of peanut butter. This was a tricky and sticky thing to eat with my neck-brace on. By the end of it my hand was covered in melted ice-cream and I was so thirsty I couldn't finish the cone because I was afraid I wouldn't be able to swallow it without choking on it. Safety first people.

Another constant there was the cleaning lady. Every morning she would knock and enter (with no pause between) and say good morning to me. She learned my name immediately and didn't forget it. She was a sweet Spanish lady with squeaky shoes and a receding hairline which was emphasized by her tight bun. Her routine to clean up my room started with taking the trash out and then wiping down my sink and toilet (even though I never used it), pulling my shades up for me and cleaning the windows. While doing all this she would talk to me in broken English. Half the time I had no idea what she said and would have to replay it in my head a few times before I could understand. She asked what happened to me one of the first days and said she would pray for me. I needed all those prayers, that is for sure. One day she mentioned how she recently lost her mother and that she missed her so much. She would always ask where my mom was if she wasn't there because she knew she came every morning. The last thing she would do was mop the floor, starting at the corner furthest from the door and working her way out of my room. Before she left she would tell me to have a good day and asked if I needed anything. I liked having her there in the morning; she brightened my day when I thought there was no way I could get up. Another reason I hated weekends- she was off duty then. I wish all the rehab personnel were like her. She did her job quickly and had a good time doing it.

Let's just face it, those student nurses are downright bothersome. And that is putting it nicely. I know their intentions are good and they're just eager to learn, but it wasn't as tolerable in such a condition as I was. Don't let the word student throw you off, they were of all ages, shapes, and sizes. The only thing that tied them together as a group was the fact that they had to wear the same ugly white uniform and had classes together. They were usually there for the evening shift, coming in at 4pm and leaving by 11pm. I knew this because they'd come into my room with their new shiny stethoscopes and blood pressure checker things and interrupt while I was watching Oprah. And by watching I mean falling asleep. Usually it wasn't too bad, but some days they thought it was a great conversation starter and would feel free to blab on and on. I didn't want to be rude so I did engage with them, but seriously, could they not sense that I was exhausted and didn't want to chit chat and make a friend? I guess they were so into the fact that they finally were working on real live patients and not just sitting in a classroom. There was no opt out button or box to select either. One student nurse would come in every hour to check on me and ask if she could do anything. She was bent on getting me cleaned up and in my pajamas and ready for bed. I told her time after time that my mom was there to do that and we didn't need any more hands in the pot. Night after night she would come in and ask. At one point she was giving me my evening medicines. This took a million times longer when she did it. Yes, I had a lot, but we had had a process down. With the student they would have to go one by one and mark it off as they went along and document it precisely. Heaven forbid there was a mistake or change in dosage; we would have to wait and start over. She had to go back to her instructor for approval and go back to the pharmacy (which was a machine) and re-enter all my info and all that jazz. The thing about it was that the student nurses were less important in the eyes of the permanent nurses and were treated as such. They were cut off in line and made to wait. Not fair to them or the patient. On the other hand, the student nurses were more likely to help if you needed something. I tricked one student nurse. I was on a diet restriction because of the blockage in my guts and was only allowed to have ice chips. Plain 'ole ice chips. They were more like little bunny turds. I couldn't even drink the water they left behind as they melted. I convinced her to put some juice over the ice chips. And to throw away the evidence. It was a little bit of heaven in my mouth when I ate those flavored chips. I even managed to sneak in a few sips of the liquids too! Karma came back though. It was when I was having some major issues with my digestion and I had to have quite a good number of enemas. Yes, the bowel flusher, as it's referred to. Well, the student nurse's assignment that one evening was to give me one. It was her first. Go figure. She told me that she had to wait for her instructor to finish up with someone and then they'd be in to give it to me. Once I found out that the instructor had to be present I knew it could not be good. They came in and the instructor walked her through the first part. She ended up taking over at one point because the student didn't know what she was doing and was taking way way way too long. I usually don't mind those things, but they seemed to go quickly and be less painful all the other times I had them done.

Sustained clonus was a piece of the aftermath. Clonus means violent, confused motion. That seemed to sum up how I was feeling about life. I still felt in shock and definitely did not know what I was going to do about what had happened. My right leg muscles were acting very weird and would not relax so it looked as if I was constantly pointing my foot. Randomly the groups of muscles would spasm and contract in ways that were not meant to occur. I could not control it. It happens frequently when there is nerve damage and the feedback is interrupted.They had to put a boot brace on it so that my leg was in a proper position for healing purposes. I would wear it while I was lying in bed, but during therapy or times when I didn't have it on my foot would just start to twitch and spasm. It wasn't always painful, just annoying because I wasn't able to consciously control it. In the mornings it was triggered a lot when I stretched. It seemed like the stretch wouldn't end and my leg would just get stuck and hyper-extend all on its own. That was painful. If I would go over a bump while in my wheelchair it was triggered or when I started putting weight on it. My doctor tried to regulate it with some medications but they only seemed to take the edge off of it. My spinal cord injury was a lot more extensive and complicated than I imagined. While that was going on, I was experiencing impairment of proprioception. It started all over my body and I couldn't properly detect where my limbs were. It would feel like my legs were up in the air when they were straight out in front of me on the bed. Or my arms often felt like I had them shoved and bent up behind my back with my hands in fists when they were straight out next to me. I had my mom move the body part in question so that I could see it with my own eyes and make the connection as to where it was at the moment. It also seemed the more it was touched the easier it was for me to feel where it truly was at that moment. We worked on that for a significant amount of time when we first began the therapy. It felt as if I was constantly sitting in a crooked position or that one hip was higher than the other. To adjust this they would help me sit up and put a huge mirror in front of me to see that I was sitting straight and relearn and reconnect how I felt my body and where it actually was. I hated when they brought the mirror out. I didn't want to see myself. I hadn't showered for so long and wasn't wearing a bra and just felt disgusting. It was bad enough I felt it, I didn't want to have to see it. Lucky for me I wasn't wearing my glasses for the first few weeks and my vision was all messed up from the medications so when I looked in the mirror it was hard for me to make out the details. I just saw enough of my outline to allow my brain to connect with my body and improve my posture and for my muscles began to feel like they were in the right position. As time went on it lessened throughout my body and remained slightly in my right arm.

At one point I looked like I was six months pregnant. The blockage in my digestive system was the culprit. As my belly became more and more swollen my appetite dwindled to nothing. The doctors said it was all of the drugs I was taking that basically over-relaxed my system to the point that it wasn't able to do the job of digesting and moving my food along. Some days it was so bad that mom would sit next to me and rub my stomach clock-wise to get things moving. I think that discomfort brought pain to a whole different level. I would have killed for them to let me take beano. I felt like I was so bloated and gassy that if I could just take some I would get relief. A few days after the surgery, we called a friend of mine in Baltimore who was planning on coming to see me, and asked him to bring some beano. He smuggled in the economy size bottle! The only issue was that I didn't want it to react with any of the other medications I was on so I was too chicken to take any. What a bummer. They didn't resolve the problem while I was in recovery in Baltimore. I was there for eight days and still had no bowel movement and even worse, I had no gas. They just loaded me up on more laxatives and stool softeners hoping they would eventually work. It went on and on and still nothing was happening. It got to a point where they put me on an IV and put me on a food and liquid restriction. The first day I was not allowed to have any food or drink. Not even water or ice. They gave my mom this square little sponge on the end of a wooden stick and told her she could soak it and dab my lips with it. That was pure torture. I would suck the water out of it anyways. The next few days I had to stay with the IV in order to get the nutrients I needed and they took me off all the narcotics and other pain medicines that I was swallowing and putting through my stomach. They gave me a pain patch instead. At first they had me on the lowest dose possible and I was still in a lot of pain, so at that point they increased the strength and let it work its magic. I was allowed ice the day after. I thought nothing tasted better than ice. It was the strangest feeling, equating ice to one of the most amazing things in the world. My stomach issues were still there. The rehab doctor decided he needed a specialist to come in and asked a GI doc to examine me. He came at night and I barely remember it. I wasn't wearing my glasses because of all the medicine they had me on; they made my eyes hurt and I would get headaches and blurriness if I wore them. I know he was Italian because of his last name. I recall he had some dark glasses on. He asked me questions and pushed around on my guts. I guess he was concerned with the situation because he told me to stay with the course of action we were on (no food) until I had a bowel movement. But the catch was that if I didn't crap in the next few days they were going to have to send me to the emergency room and put a NG tube down my throat to get rid of the blockage so that it would not cause any of my organs to burst. Oh great. Instead of focusing on that, I would find myself joking with the nurses the next day because they told me I got the cute doctor to come in. It was funny to me because I couldn't even see him. After a couple of days nothing changed. One morning I was feeling super bad and had some major pains in my guts. I looked over at my mom and said that I didn't feel well. She hit the call nurse button because she thought something wasn't right and wanted someone to check me. All of a sudden I was lying in my bed and I started to vomit. My mom with her fast reactions turned me to my side so I wouldn't choke on my own puke and just held me in that position while I barfed all over the bed and floor and mom. I felt better but that was a mess. I thought I saw black stuff in my vomit but attributed it to my vision issues. But then I was told that I had just thrown up crap that was backed up in my system for the past couple of weeks. Poop chunks out of the mouth, now isn't that attractive? It was a good thing I threw up though, the GI doctor came back in to examine me and told me if I went one more day they were going to have to intervene. Now that I got rid of that, I was allowed soft foods. This was torture too. I never though I would be so sick of chocolate pudding and cherry jello. I had a hard time eating that crap and the nutritionist had to come and talk to me. I told her what I was allowed and not allowed to eat and then the choices that were available for me to eat. She realized I had some slim pickings and went on a mission for me. She brought back my very own fruit drink things that were chock full of the vitamins and minerals and proper food servings that I needed. It went like this for another couple of weeks. Once I started to have regular bowel movements they re-evaluated me to see if I could start incorporating solids back into my diet. I was craving things so badly. When I would watch television any food commercial would get my stomach going. There were very weird ones too; normally I hate eating lunch meats and especially ham, but I wanted a ham and cheese sandwich with mustard on white bread-the kind that sticks to the roof of your mouth. I had to fight with them to allow me to have my rice crispies back when I was cleared for some solids. There was a miscommunication and they thought I was banned solids because I would choke on them. They didn't realize it was due to my digestion. I fought for several days to get those for breakfast. I would have them written on my menu and if they weren't on my tray I'd ask a nurse or someone to go get them. Most of the time I was denied, but I still tried my hardest.

They had me on a fentanyl patch once I was in rehab. Every two days they were changing the patch and the nurses would have to sign off on it and throw it away a special way so that no one would go through the trash and take it out to use whatever was left on the patch after it had been on my skin for 48 hours. I had developed a dependency on the patch and was trying to wean myself off of it but my withdrawal symptoms were very overwhelming. I would get super anxious, have a runny nose and goose bumps, muscle spasms, shivering, and sweating. I would just lay on the couch and try to calm myself and sleep it off but that usually did not happen. I would have to cover up with blankets and put a heating pad on wherever I could just to help me relax. I had to resort to self-medicating and using my valium and other muscle spasm medicines to counteract the withdrawal symptoms. The worst part of it all was waiting for the drugs to kick in. Once they did it was all okay. Just those twenty to thirty minutes of torture and then it would subside.

I didn't shower for 4 weeks. They had these hair cap things that you warm up and then rub it all on your hair and it's supposed to clean your hair. Sometimes, it actually made my hair feel even worse than it did before the cap treatment. I was happy with daily birdbaths. It gave me anxiety just to think of the process that it would involve- switching braces, letting the nurses carry me to the shower chair and keep me balanced while giving me a shower. My mom asked me to take one for her birthday present. There wasn't much more I could do for her, so I sucked it up and agreed. After it was done and over with she asked me if it was as bad as I thought it would be. Yes, it was just as bad as I had imagined. I felt fresh and shiny afterwards, but the whole idea of it still freaked me out. The risk did not seem greater than the reward at the time. I was super paranoid my neck would get turned or my head would fall off or my back would get whacked out. It was unlikely, but at that point in my life anything was possible. I was scarred from the surgery and my unpreparedness of the outcome.

Breakfast in bed brought on a whole new meaning for those 7 long weeks. When I first arrived I wasn't even able to feed myself and so I was able to just sit in my hospital bed and have mom (or a nurse) feed me. I had many mornings where I just couldn't eat and was sick. The menu came daily and we had to select what I was going to have the next day to eat. This was always hard because it usually had to be filled out when I was least hungry and nothing was appetizing. At first the selection seemed impressive to me, but as I stayed longer I saw how it just rotated. Over and over. Bananas were a staple and at one point I was hooked on rice crispies. I had a system down to eat the cereal- it's quite difficult to do with a neck brace on. The bed didn't sit up all the way and I couldn't sit up on my own, so I ate in a slight recline... danger! One end of the napkin was tucked into my brace right under my chin and the other end I tucked right under whatever I was eating. When I was done with my cereal there was usually more on my napkin than in my mouth. My hand was very shaky and it would spill milk off the spoon and onto the napkin with every bite. Instead of a milk mustache I would develop a milk beard. Dinner was also in my room. Mom usually brought me food from home that she made, but I liked to snack so we still selected things from the menu (usually the sweets). After a few weeks when I was able to finally use a fork and bring it to my mouth on my own the OT and Nurse wanted me to start eating in the cafeteria with everyone else. I refused. This was a huge issue for me at the time, no compromise from me.

It was bad enough that I had to eat lunch every day in that cafeteria with everyone. All they did was complain and ask each other what they were in for and how long. And since the majority were over the age of 70 they had to talk loud. The nurses were assigned to stand and watch us. I needed help opening and cutting things so they would do that for me. I took my time when I ate and was almost always the last patient sitting there. I ended up making friends with the staff. They'd come out of the kitchen and hang around to clean up. One day, they had just baked cookies for later that evening. I heard them talking about it and I wanted one so I ate as slow as possible and when the nurse came to bring me back to my room I asked her for one... jackpot! It's amazing how something like getting a fresh cookie from the oven can make your day. The nurse on duty knew my routine and after every lunch I would ask for a coffee and she'd get that for me and sit with me for a few minutes before I'd have to go back to the hell hole gym and do therapy. If the weather was nice out the nurse would let me eat outside on the patio. This was the hot spot for all the nurses. They had to eat their lunch somewhere. Most of them were younger, well, all were younger than the patients, so it was nice to be in company with them. I ended up getting the worst farmers tan from eating out there, but it was well worth it.

The icepack trick was a very important one and my therapists would have it all ready for me when I needed it. I felt off kilter and like I was leaning and sitting on my right side more than my left. I didn't know if it was because of the paralysis or because my back was now straight and I just had to get familiar with the new position. Well, either way, after sitting up for more than an hour the butt bone on my right side would throb and throb. It would start to make my whole leg hurt. From trying to shift around so much with my left side then that would start to hurt. The wheelchair they had me sitting in wasn't really for sensitive pressure points. So they had these packs (hot or cold, take your pick) and you would simply pop them and shake them up and they would get hot or cool instantly! For my buns I chose cold. I would have the nurse or therapist shove those things right under my butt. It was instant relief. Plus, once it was no longer cold, it still provided some cushioning under there. Those were another thing we hoarded in my closet. Good thing because we went through those like crazy and sometimes there was a shortage. Not a good thing. One day the trick just wasn't cutting it for me. It was a Friday so I was already exhausted from the week full of therapy. Plus, I was miserable because it was the end of the day and that meant it was the weekend. I had been sitting in my wheelchair all day long and was in a lot of pain. I got back to my room and buzzed my nurse in. I asked if they could put me back in my bed because my butt was killing me and the icepack wasn't working. She told me she had to go and find another nurse to help her lift me in. Ten minutes went by. And then another ten. I pushed the call button again. She finally came in and told me that they wanted me to stay in my wheelchair and out of my bed longer. I wish she would have just told me that in the first place. I asked her why and explained that I wanted to get back into my bed so badly, I had been upright for way too long and was getting to the point of pain beyond controlling. She offered me some tylenol. That was a joke. That did squat. So, I used my invalid card. I called her back and told her I had to go to the bathroom. I still was unable to move so they had to put me back in bed to help me go on the bed pan. I knew they couldn't deny me of that. Otherwise they would have a mess on their hands which was a lot worse- peeing right there on my wheelchair and all over my clothes and the floor. It did happen once. I didn't try it. I thought I could hold it longer than I was really able to and it just came out and wouldn't stop. Not only did they have to clean me up, but they had to deal with the dirty chair and wet pee floor in my room. So she really did get someone this time to help her with getting me in bed and taken care of. It worked and I could finally relax and release the pressure not only on my butt but also my bladder. I was definitely gladder. That nurse was just following orders probably from the therapy department to make me stay in my chair longer but that wasn't fair to her because then she had to deal directly with me and I was in no mood. It made me very mad that she just didn't fess up in the first place when I asked to get back in bed. Instead she led me on and told me she would go and find someone to help her when in fact she was just seeing how long I really would put up with staying in my chair. It made me frustrated because I couldn't do anything about the situation like just getting up and plopping into bed and be lazy. I had to use my manipulation skills and figure out another way to get around the problem. I became very savvy with those kinds of things. There is always more than one solution to a problem.

Nighttime was not a fun time for me. I happened to be put in a room right by the nurses station. This was good for the times when I couldn't feel my call bell and had to yell for the nurse. For all other purposes it wasn't that great. They seemed to like to talk as loud as possible and act like teenagers into the wee hours of the morning. They didn't do as much as the day shift so I guess they were left to think of ways to entertain themselves for their 8 hours. Yes, I could've closed the door, but then I wouldn't have been heard if I needed to get help and I couldn't push my call button. I had to have someone come in at least every 3 hours to turn me or help me use the bedpan. There was one nurse that landed on the shit list the first week I was there. He came in when I rang the bell to help me with the bedpan and rolling me. I knew I had to pee, but once I was actually on the bedpan I couldn't go. I asked him to give me a few minutes. The next thing I know, I am waking up and trying to figure out what was going on. It was when I was still given lots of narcotics so I drifted in and out and had a hard time keeping up with things going on. My body was still very numb. I couldn't remember if I actually had been put on the bedpan or if I just was having a dream about it. So I tried to feel if there was something under me, but couldn't move my arms so I called the nurse back in. I told him when he walked in how I couldn't figure out if there was a bedpan under my butt or not. He acted a bit strangely and that is when I realized I wasn't dreaming, I was rolled onto it 3 hours ago!! I had semi-permanent bedpan lines on me. They had to peel the thing off me and put cream on the areas where it dug into me. After that incident I mentioned it to my head nurse the next morning and from then on out they had the night shifters checking in on me every 2 hours. I didn't see too much of that nurse afterwards either, I think he was transferred to another area of the rehab.

Luckily we could control the thermostat to my room. One of the perks I guess you could say. Those old people love cranking the heat up. My room was always the coolest room in the building the nurses would tell me. I would rather have it freezing in my room and just bundle up with blankets than to have it like a sauna. If I wanted heat and humidity I would just ask someone to take me outside. I guess having a neck-brace on made me feel suffocated enough. The regulation mattered the most at night. It was tricky too, literally one degree up or down could determine whether it was going to be an icebox or a Bikram yoga studio. A few times I found myself waking up with a nose that was stuffy and I would be soaked in sweat and felt like I couldn't breathe. I would just ring the nurse bell and they would turn it down for me. After about twenty minutes my room cooled off and my nose cleared up and I was able to feel more comfortable. Sweating was one of the worst things when I had that brace on. I was ripe enough when I wasn't sweating.

One Friday afternoon, I had a wonderful surprise. Three of my cousins popped their heads into my room! I started to cry, which is not very like me. They drove all the way from Massachusetts to visit me for the weekend. I was so happy, weekends were usually miserable and very much dreaded. Actually, I hated weekends in there. It was like a ghost town. It was so boring and depressing I would go into the gym and do exercises on my own. So when I actually had my cousins to enjoy a weekend with it was all good in my world. I couldn't believe they were there! We just hung out in the room for a bit. I was super tired from the meds and the therapy I had to do that day. They left after a bit to get dinner and then made their way back that evening with my parents and Uncle Steve and Auntie M. We had a party in my room! It was so weird to have all these people around. I was on overload for sure. I dozed in and out a few times I'm sure and I tried my best to stay up, but my body didn't want to cooperate. That was one of the best nights I had and it was very much needed. My heart and soul were light and smiling that night. I had my cousins to look forward to the next day!

It's a good thing they were around, the weather was so depressing, cold and cloudy. I needed fresh air desperately, so they bundled me up and we hung outside on the patio. Dad even came by with Manu. We got him to sit on my lap. I wasn't able to pet him yet, but I think he knew instinctively that it was me, just not the same. I didn't want him to go, but since they wouldn't allow pets in the building he wasn't able to come in. I was freezing and it was really starting to make my nerves angry, so we moved our visit back into my room. Sarah attempted to paint my nails for me, but I still couldn't tell where my right arm was and I couldn't move my left arm that much so it was a bit of a challenge. We did it though and it didn't go unnoticed, my therapists complimented the whole next week.

I had my laptop in my closet so we pulled it out and skyped Rose and Mick. We were having a great time and making lots of noise, one nurse poked her head in to see what was going on. I thought she was going to yell at us for being too loud, but she just smiled and closed the door. I was thankful that she understood how much I needed that silliness and company of my family.

They went back to my house in the afternoon to let me rest, which was much needed. I hadn't had that much activity since my surgery! They came back with dinner and my parents. I had a mini melt down when my mom and dad were getting me from my bed to the chair. It was the first time they did it together and the first time my dad did it period. That alone made me nervous, but the fact that they were arguing about it before we even started to move me was even worse. I had been having extreme spasms in my stomach and guts lately whenever I was moved. It was excruciating pain and made me so on edge whenever I had to be put in my chair. They shifted me and lifted me into my chair but I sat on my arm and my legs dropped from the bed and wacked into my wheelchair. Neither hurt of course because I couldn't feel it, but it was all that needed to happen for yet another fight to break out between the two. Blaming each other. My guts did the spasm thing and I just started bawling my eyes out for a few minutes. I made a quick recovery and was good to go. I don't know exactly why I cried but it was needed to release some stress and anxiousness. Embarrassing for me to cry like that in front of everyone, but it just happened and I couldn't control it. Everyone gave me a few minutes and after some consolation from mom I was done with the breakdown. That was that and we moved on with our evening. We reserved the family room and my mom set up a fabulous spaghetti dinner. She went all out with the homemade sauce that tastes like heaven and her delicious garlic bread that was to die for. Real food, finally. The pasta was a challenge to eat, I went through about five napkins. Even though I did my bib trick, I tucked one end into my neck brace right under my chin and the other end under my plate so it was like a catch-all, it seemed to fail more than usual. I just shoveled the pasta in my mouth so maybe that is why. It was too heavy for the napkin to hold. I have never had so much sauce all over my face. We even had a pie with bananas, can't go wrong with that. And to top it all off we had our coffee. It was so much fun to get out of my bed and have conversation for longer than five minutes. My poor dad was surrounded by five girls gabbing his ears off. He is used to that and I am positive he finds it entertaining and maybe even enjoyable. I was having a hard time by the end of the night being in that wheelchair for so long, my butt was killing me. Even with the icepack trick. It was time to retreat back into the hospital bed. It was sad to say goodbye to my cousins, but my exhaustion made it quite easy. I enjoyed it while it lasted.

7 DO I HAVE TO GO BACK THERE?

Six weeks after my surgery I had to go back down to Baltimore to have a follow-up visit with the surgeon. I guess it's protocol; I sure knew it wasn't his concern for my well-being that he was seeing me. If anything he wanted to make sure I wasn't digressing so that he could sleep better at night for messing things up.

I was nervous about how I was going to be transported because I still was not able to move enough for one person to get me in and out of my wheelchair let alone a vehicle. Luckily, the staff at rehab already had it all planned out and coordinated with a transportation service. It was a relief to know my mom wouldn't have to worry about getting me there on my own.

I was excited for several reasons to have this appointment. First, it got me out of therapy for the day. Second, I was given a boxed lunch that they made and was able to grab all the snacks and drinks I wanted from the cafeteria. And third, it allowed me to leave that building for the first time in five weeks. All those things were offset with just the thought of having to face my surgeon. I had no clue what he would say to me, it could be words of criticism that I wasn't working hard enough or taking it easy, or that I was as far as I could get in my recovery. I didn't want to hear his sly remarks or idiotic humor. When it came down to it, I simply wanted him to be humble and admit that something horrible went wrong and tell me how to fix it and get back to where I was before I was laying in that bed unable to move. I was hoping he would have enough couth this time.

My mom got me as un-smelly and presentable as possible without giving me a shower. My hair wasn't too bad since I had taken one a few days before over the weekend. I wasn't dressed to impress, but my mind was far from that. I was given some medicine to help with the ride down and back, making it a lot more comfortable and less nerve-wracking. It was so nice outside, I couldn't wait to get some fresh air. The transportation arrived and turned out to be a big van with ramps and lifts and tie-backs. The driver, an older man with white hair and peaceful eyes, arrived in my room about an hour before we were scheduled to leave, but just wanted me to know he was there and was going to get a coffee and whenever I was ready we'd load up. He had a sweet spirit about him which made the trip very calm.

He packed me and my treats into the van with the blue sky surrounding me. The sun warmed me up and made my soul feel like it was soaring. I stayed in my wheelchair and he went up on a lift with me. After he rolled me into the center and put all my breaks on he started hooking me up with belts and straps to keep the chair from shifting or tilting. I was hoping they were pulled tight enough because I had no way of bracing myself for a fast stop. I knew the belt he put around me was secure, I could feel it digging into my guts. I'd rather it be like that then loose and allowing me to move all around. I was relieved to see that as he was pulling the straps to secure my wheelchair that his arm muscles were straining and neck vain popping.

As we ventured out I could feel my medicine kicking in and was able to just sit there and relax, as long as I didn't watch the road or when we braked behind cars I was feeling fine. I was super sleepy so I started to doze off. Mom sat up front with our driver and they chit-chatted the whole way down. Towards the end of the drive my butt was really starting to hurt and I needed an icepack shoved under there. I couldn't shift to my side or switch positions so it was a battle to try and get my mind on anything but my discomfort.

When we arrived at the front of the hospital we were dropped off right near the entrance. Our driver was just going to park the van and then wait until we were finished. We exchanged cell phone numbers so we could call him. Up to the fifth floor mom pushed me where we checked in. The waiting room was empty and they actually called us back quickly. Before we saw the surgeon he requested for x-rays to be taken of my neck and spine. The technician was having a hard time because she didn't know how to get the pictures she needed without moving me. They tried a few different ones and had us wait while they checked to make sure they came out clear enough. It worked and we were then brought down the hallway to the same small examining room that we had been to the first time we saw him. It was still crowded with too many chairs and other non-essential medical equipment. As we waited I was thinking about not drinking any fluids so that I wouldn't have to pee. I was wearing my briefs so it's not like I'd leak all over my chair or anything, but I didn't want to sit in a pee-filled diaper either.

When the doctor finally came in he had this smirk on his face and an air about him. He didn't say much, asked questions about what I did in rehab and why I wasn't doing more than that. He wanted me in water therapy. We tried to explain to him that they couldn't accommodate that request but he just ignored whatever came out of our mouths and went to the next item on his agenda. He told me that the bone looked like it was fusing. Then my mom asked him if he wanted to check my incisions and he said not really. I don't understand this man. That would be one of the basic things to check on and it didn't take much. I leaned forward and he lifted my shirt and took one glance at the scar and said, "Boy, that scar is beautiful, you must've had an excellent surgeon". I couldn't respond to that, it was a jaw-dropping comment but mine stayed right where it was thanks to my neck brace. He told me he was happy with my progress and to keep it up. I was to see him in another six weeks to check on my fusion.

We weren't thrilled with the visit, but I wasn't really expecting anything special. I knew not to get any hopes up that he would be a decent person. The trip back was short for me since I slept the entire way. We got back after they had served dinner, but they saved me a tray. That was a draining day: being upright for so many hours, leaving rehab, and seeing the person whose hand put me in this position.

8 BREAKING OUT

The last day in rehab had finally arrived and felt unreal. I couldn't believe I was being discharged. I was happy to finally be getting out of the place but at the same time I didn't think I was ready to go home. I just learned how to walk with the walker and use the toilet. At least in rehab I had everything I needed and nurses care 24/7. A few days before I had a total breakdown during my occupational therapy session. It was right before lunch and we were in the community room practicing sitting up from laying down and vice versa. I was working with my regular therapist as well as a new therapist that was in training. She had just been hired there and started the week before. My therapist kept having me lay down and try to push myself up with one arm since my right arm was still just flopping around on its own. I couldn't do it. My brace was in the way and I couldn't push myself enough to get back into a sitting position. I was trying so hard but it wasn't enough. Tears just started falling out of my eyeballs. I wanted to give up but they wouldn't let me. We figured out if there was a big wedge foam piece under me when I was laying down I could get myself to sit up easier. But that meant I would have to go to sleep on an incline with a giant wedge beneath me, boy, does that sound like a fabulous method of sleeping. I know I was being a complete melodramatic, but it was just then hitting me that I have to go home and I won't have these conveniences of being in the hospital and it made me made feel like the hospital was better than being home at that point. I didn't have a bed that went up and down as needed or a bathroom that was as accessible or nurses on call 24/7 or a cafeteria to provide me with whatever I wanted whenever I wanted or a team of people forcing me to go to PT and OT every day or a call button or constant doctor monitoring. I was going to have to rely on my mom and that was not fair to her. This situation had already taken over our lives somewhat, now with going home it would only become more overwhelming, at least it seemed that is how it was going to be. She was already sacrificing so much of her time to care for me and do other people's jobs. It would work out and I knew that in the back of my head, but I was having a hard time reminding myself of that.

My mom brought my car for me because the seats were leather and the car was lower which made it a lot easier to get into the car. I felt like I was breaking out of jail. I was going home! It was a very weird feeling to be able to leave that place after it being my home for what felt like so long. No more walks around the building or sitting out on the back patio made of cobblestone which was so ignorant since wheelchairs had to go across it or watching the cars and trucks pass by on the highway or walk by the hospice next door and admire the beautiful landscaping and gazebo that they had that we were not allowed to enjoy. I wouldn't have to listen to the constant ringing of people's call bells for the nurses or moaning from crazy Deb. I was going to be able to sleep in my own bed and not be required to wake up early every morning. It felt like I had never been in a car before. Every movement made me nervous that I was going to hurt something. It was not a bright sunny day, but it was warm enough that we could have the windows down and air blowing through. That was something I missed a lot. My eyes had to adjust to the brightness, I was so used to the indoors and the horrible fluorescent lighting. Once we pulled up to the house I was very excited to see Manu. I was hoping he wouldn't jump on me and make me loose my balance. Mom put me in my wheelchair and rolled me across the grass to our side porch. We had a portable (and very steep) ramp to get my wheelchair up and onto the porch. From there we had to maneuver up one stair through the door and there I was- home sweet home. It was so nice to be in my house. I was extremely worn out from the day, my body was not used to that much activity and stimulation! We headed right up to my bedroom. She basically lifted me up the stairs and helped me scoot onto my bed. I didn't have a giant wedge to lay against so she just helped me lay back and got me all comfortable. And this is where Manu came bounding in so excited, tail wagging a mile a minute. He ran up the little doggy steps I have so that he can get on my bed on his own and laid right on my chest and stomach and would not stop licking me. He was so happy I was there and he could lay with me. We took a nap together for a good chunk of time

One of the last nights in rehab I spent a few hours searching for new sneakers to buy on Zappos. This website was on my radar before it became famous.

Before they could afford to do commercials on television. Before they were a clue and answer on Jeopardy! I had discovered this fabulous website where you could buy shoes by all different criteria (color, type, heel height, etc) but that wasn't the best part. There was no shipping OR return shipping fees! It's hard to find any types of shoes my size that don't have glitter or Disney characters on them. When I was able to find age-appropriate shoes in my size I knew I hit the jackpot. I ended up ordering about 20 pairs of shoes to try on. When I got home there was the giant-sized box of shoes. My Uncle was over and helped me to try every single pair on. It was very entertaining. Gave me something to do with my time! I chose one pair and we shipped all the rest back. I can always guarantee entertainment with Zappos. I have bought almost all of my shoes from this company. I guess I am such a frequent buyer that they usually upgrade my shipping to overnight for free! If I put bumper stickers on the back of my car, I would put their logo there. But, I hate bumper stickers, so that won't happen. I don't like to show off what I believe in or love or get annoyed with on the back of my car for complete strangers to read and draw a conclusion from. Mind your own business and keep your eyes on the road. There are too many times where I catch myself reading someone's bumper stick and pay more attention to that instead of what is going on around me and more importantly, the road.

The cost of this whole thing is astronomical. I am blessed to have insurance that covers it. How do people who don't have insurance do it? If it weren't for my parents not charging me rent or making me buy my own food I would surely be in the streets. My benefit statements would come in the mail and had the breakdown of what everything was costing. I've reached almost a half million dollars with this. The hospital and staff and equipment and medications and on and on. I'd be bankrupt if I was expected to pay all of this out of my own pockets. I am positive I will hit a million dollars in costs by the time I am thirty. Sure, there are deductibles and such, but hey, it's not even close to what I would have to pay if there was no insurance coverage. I was under my dad's insurance plan until I graduated from college. He never once complained about any medical costs or anything having to do with money and my disability. Never brought it up in front of me at least. Whatever I needed to function (wheelchair, walker, crutches, ramp, etc.) he never questioned and let me handle it. Thank goodness. I think I would be very bitter towards my father if he ever held that over my head. In rehab I had to start thinking about Long Term Disability and Social Security and COBRA. Things I was definitely not prepared to do and think about. I would have a long time period where I would have no income between the gap of the short and long term disability pay. I would have to try and defer my college loans and put aside enough for health care and other expenses that would not be included in my insurance. When I was home I received a bill from rehab (about six months after my surgery). I opened it and all I saw was the $400,000 that was owed to my doctor. I was stunned and I am pretty sure my mouth dropped and my face turn bright red with annoyance, my ears were surely on fire. I hated dealing with the insurance companies and the medical bills and the complete disconnect that occurs between the two. I would say 75% of the time I don't feel it's necessary to follow-up with my insurance to make sure they are paying the correct amount and/or correct person. However, once in a blue moon it is quite possible they messed up and it must be looked into and addressed. This would be one of those situations. I was not about to be responsible for $400,000 of medical care. How was I going to pay that ever in my lifetime?! I know some companies accept a monthly pay plan, but it would take me 4,000 months to pay that off if they agreed to let me pay $100 monthly. That is almost 77 years. I am not planning on living until I am 102 years old. At least I know I won't have any kids that will have to pay it if I died with a balance. It is always a mystery who to call first and how to go about disputing something like this, but it had to be done and either way there is going to be a lot of back and forth nonsense that is unavoidable. Nothing is simple when an insurance company is involved.

In the end I had to call the rehab to find out what this bill was for and why I was receiving it and if I really did have to pay it. It was through them that I discovered it was my rehab doctor that I had to pay somehow. He ended up not being covered under my plan. I was thrown for a loop on that one because I had made sure that the rehab was covered by my insurance plan. I had to call the insurance company and they confirmed that my rehab was covered, but the doctor that treated me while I was there was independent of the rehab place and his claim was denied because he was not covered by my plan. Here is the catch: he was the only doctor there and I had no other choice available. The insurance company then had to open a case and research and investigate what the situation was and who would get paid and how. It took almost a year, but in the end, my insurance company covered this out-of-network doctor because at the rehab he was the only doctor and this qualified as an exception to the typical terms. That was a major relief to know that I didn't half to come up with half a million dollars.

The whole entire house had to be adapted so that I could be home. All the rugs had to come up. A new railing was installed on the left side of the stairs since my right arm couldn't function with the railing on the right. A lower table was brought into the dining room so I could reach when I ate. A portable toilet was put in the living room so I could go to the bathroom without going up the stairs. To preserve my privacy mom found a screen room divider type thing that blocked the area off so that whenever I went I wasn't out in the open for everyone to see. A ramp was put on the side porch so my walker could go right up. Lots of dresses were bought because I had a hard time pulling up my underwear or pants. My bed was taken off of the frame so that it was lower and I didn't have to struggle and climb into it. I had to get a tupperware container to fit all of my drugs in with labels. There were medical supplies everywhere: neck brace pads, odds and ends to make my brace more comfortable, different size pillows for different occasions whether it be on the porch or sitting on the couch or a chair, wheelchair, walker, crutches, canes

The day after I returned home from rehab, visitors arrived. This was slightly nighmare-ish. The timing was horrible. Mom and I hadn't even gotten a schedule down or things figured out yet. The day before I slept from the afternoon until evening. The only thing we figured out was my medications, first things first. We had stopped on the way home at the Pharmacy to get the goods. It was a couple of large bags that was handed through the drive-through window, who knows what the pharmacist thought. We needed a rolling suitcase to transport them all! The nerve pain meds, my pain patches, valium, spasm meds, laxative/stool softener, and all of the drugs I was taking pre-surgery. We made a schedule so that we didn't miss a dose. Otherwise, I would have withdrawal symptoms which were not fun. That first night was hard, I had to call my mom's name every two hours so that she could come and help me turn to a different side. I would barely be awake to do this, but she would get out of bed and come in my room to shift me. I would fall back to sleep as if I didn't even wake up. I am sure my mom could only sleep lightly, if that, because in the back of her head she didn't want to not hear me calling for her.

The most difficult thing at night was if I had to pee. I couldn't just hold it and wait until the morning, my bladder wasn't that strong yet. We had the port-a-pot in my room so I wouldn't have to walk too far to go. After all that I slept in pretty late-9am versus 7am in rehab. Later that afternoon the family arrived. I had not been feeling well when I got up, my stomach was unhappy and I hadn't gone to the bathroom for a couple of days now. My bloated belly was a solid rock. This was when I could say I was full of crap literally. I tried to at least have a bit of toast and fruit because my medications I take suggest to take them only with food. I ate as much as I could, but I was feeling worse so I went to lay on the couch while they all finished up with their breakfast. After a few minutes I decided to try and sit on my toilet in the living room behind the asian inspired screen. I sat and sat. Nothing. I was getting soar from just hanging out there and still no change in my nausea. My mom helped me back to the coach. She took one look at my paled green face and knew what was coming. I was able to keep it in my mouth while she ran to get a bowl and everyone else around tried to help but ended up just getting in the way. Mom and I had it handled while I barfed my guts out. It is very difficult to throw up with a neck brace on, all I could do was hope that it wouldn't get on my brace pads. That would be disgusting. We got through that dilemma and I just had to lay on the couch for a bit. I didn't know what to do because we had guests and it wasn't like they were able to come visit anytime as if they lived around the corner.

The next few months I was home-bound. Traveling was very difficult and uncomfortable. Most of the days I spent out of the porch or sleeping. I had to lay down a lot during the day to relieve the pressure of the brace on my jaw/shoulders and butt. The medications I was on also caused a lot of drowsiness. I would start to go cross-eyed or have blurry vision or even a hard time keeping my eyelids open. My eyeballs would feel like they were swollen and going to pop out of my head! I had to learn to write with my left hand and to practice on that I'd work on sudoku and crossword puzzles. Once I had a bit more control with my left arm and felt awake enough I read a lot. That's something that could entertain me for hours. There was even a local bookstore that gave me a bag full of books that were based on a list I had made of recently read books that I enjoyed. Other than that, I had therapy. That alone was like a full-time job. Not only was I exercising when they came to the house but I was given things to work on in between. I was told I had eighteen months to get back into shape and whatever condition my nerves were in at that point is how they would most likely be for the rest of my life. That was a constant threat in my mind. I was against the clock.

We were able to have a visiting nurse/therapy/aide service come to the house. I found one that my insurance would cover and was able to have the OT and PT come out to work with me twice a week each. I also had a personal aide come once a week to help with showering and laundry and things like that. All because I was considered home bound. I wasn't able to go out of the house on my own or even if someone was with me it still was very difficult. Somehow, I was sent the best team of therapists I had for a long time. I wasn't used to working one-on-one with a therapist all to myself for a whole hour. It was amazing. We were able to assess what I needed to work on, they'd help me do things I couldn't do on my own like stretching, and they give me things to do until they came the next time. They were very creative in their approaches and really seemed to help set reasonable goals. We would use things around the house to help challenge me. They would find out what I liked to do and we'd put a spin on it so that it was exercise but not dreadful. We started from scratch and did things that made sense, not just a plan that was designed for the general population and assigned to me. That is very important to me because I do not have a typical or average body. Mine functions in a very unique way. It's a mystery when it comes to the best way of doing things, trial and error. For the most part I am definitely up to trying different and new and difficult things, but I have to listen to my body and if it doesn't feel right more damage could be done.

Delores was one of my most entertaining aides ever. Well, I've only had a few, but I could confidently surmise that she pretty much rocked. I never felt awkward or nervous or embarrassed around her, and her job duties she was responsible for were the one that would make you think the opposite- she was my own personal cleaner.

That would be from head to toe. We didn't have her at the house right away, but once we found out that I was covered to have an aide she came one or two times a week. I had her come every day when my mom was off in Italy. It was a good thing she came along. My mom was completely burnt out from having to take care of me. She was so tired and exhausted but would always push through and put me first. Delores and I made arrangements to come one morning and we did this through texting. Strange, but it worked. She showed up to my house with her white hair pulled back into a long braid. She was very petite, but I know from experience there was some hidden strength inside somewhere. I did not expect my texting aide to be a cute old lady. I hope she wasn't texting and driving. We picked out what I was going to wear- I sat on my bed and she went through my armoire picking out whatever I wanted. I normal would just be waking up so she made sure to let me lay there as long as possible and would set the bathroom up while I rested. Once it was all ready she would help me into the bathroom. At first this involved my walker and then I would sit on the side of the tub while she made more room in the bathroom by putting the walker in the hallway. We would take out my bathroom tub thing that we took from rehab that was supposed to be a water basin I guess. It worked just as good as a catch-all for my supplies. We had everything in there from powder to toothpaste and spit tray. We got a routine down by the second time. She would help me get undressed and we switched to my water neck brace. This alternate brace was only to be worn when showering because it is just a piece of foam that velcros to itself in the back. It was heavenly to have that suffocating neck brace off for a few seconds while we switched to the water one. My jaw felt like it wasn't able to stay closed since it didn't sit the same on the edge of the brace. All of my muscles were going to crap. She would help me swing my legs over the tub wall and keep me from falling over. I would shift over to my shower seat and we would get all situated.

She sang. It put me at ease and was very humorous. She would make lyrics up to older tunes like, "She'll be comin' round the mountain". From start to finish she would sing. And while she helped to wash me up, she would name the different parts she would clean and then tell me the stories behind them. She told me that the armpits are the "stinkies" because she once had a lady who was Spanish and could not speak much English and Delores was told by this lady that is what armpits were called. The other names included "suzy jane" and "hinnerdale". The best thing about Delores is that she would always tell stories but could work at the same time. If there was a picture next to an entertaining and helpful, efficient person in the dictionary it would be a head shot of Delores. She would powder and lotion me up and help with brushing my teeth and getting my brace back on and putting my clothes on- all of this while having a blast with me. The best thing about her was that the next time she came, she knew exactly what to do and where to go and how to help me. I didn't have to remind her constantly of what I needed and could or could not do. She had her job down to a science and even better was that she truly did care about me. It was not just a job to her, she understood that what she was doing for me made the world a whole different place, not just for me, but she was a huge relief for mom when she was there. She even cleaned out the port-a-pot for me when she was there. Before she left she would make sure I had everything I needed and would set me up with food and drink if I asked. It was strange to me that I was that comfortable around her and what she did for me. I never had a moment of awkwardness with her and she always was able to brighten my morning.

The occupational therapist they sent to the house was a fun lady too. Jackie was in her late thirties and had been in this field for her entire career, so she knew what she needed to do and for the things she wasn't familiar with she would ask. Her voice was very cheerful, sometimes too much because she would come in the morning time-frame and sometimes early enough that I wasn't even out of bed. She was a bright and nurturing therapist. Her goals with me were to adapt whatever I needed around the house and to get my right arm functioning and my left arm strong. To start off she asked me what I couldn't do and what I wanted to do and what I was capable of before the surgery. She wanted to know what my typical day and night were like. She asked what my goals were. She was taking notes while we went over all of those details and gathered enough information to write up a plan of action for the next session. She took measurements of how far I could lift and bend my arm and also how tightly I could squeeze. Every few sessions we would refer back to those numbers and see if there was any improvement and also to see which I needed to work more on. She would give me assignments that I would have to do every day and even some a few times a day in between her visits. That is where the rice bowl came in to play. She wanted to help desensitize my nerves that were going haywire. She also hooked me up with some putty like the one I used to work with in rehab. The difference was that she just asked me to squeeze it in my hand and rotate, like those china town balls that you move in your palms that come in a little box. She would come to the house two times a week.

Len was my physical therapist. I am not sure how he could know all the information he knew and still understand how to present it to me in a way that I could grasp what was going on. He arrived on a hot afternoon. My mom was out doing groceries and I was on the porch with my grandparents relaxing. We heard the door bell ring but I wasn't expecting anyone. My grandfather got the door and came out to tell me that my therapist was here. I was so confused because I had just seen Jackie that morning. It turned out to be this savant who sat down with me and went over what happened and the probable reasons as to why it happened. He made drawings and gave examples. He was on a clear mission to answer as many of my questions as possible. He was there to keep me on track and push me to my limits and warn me when I was doing too much.

I began collecting medical equipment. Some would say I had a slight case of hoarding if they saw my closet. It began with just a bagful of neck brace pads. Every other day we had to change the pads because they needed to be washed and the padding flattened out and I would start to get these cuts on my back and on my collar bone where the bottom of the brace would rub and dig into me. The skeleton of the brace was made of some sort of sturdy plastic with a few spots of velcro here and there for the pads to stick to. We were having to change them so frequently that my mom started to make her own from a roll that the brace lady had given us because they did not have any more precut pads. My mom took a pad and traced it around the new padding roll stuff and just cut it out of that. I had my boot that I was supposed to be wearing more frequently than I was. There were all the ace wraps we were using either on my knees or my right hand to keep them in their proper places. I bought some weights that I could wrap around my legs and wrists to continue my therapy at home. I even bought a wedge to use for when I went to bed so I could sit up and lay down with more ease. Yeah, that didn't work and didn't last for more than a minute. I was so mad too because I had asked my OT what size I should get and so I ordered that and it was just way too big. I barely had to sit back and there it was. I would not be able to sleep on that thing. One of my best friends became the donut. Not the edible kind either. We got a blow up cushion type one with a hole in the middle- the kind they give patients with hemorrhoids. It helped to relieve a ton of pressure and discomfort on my tailbone. We had a ton of gauze and cotton pads for my head wounds caused by the brace. And then once therapy started at home I accrued even more. Homemade exercising stuff was around, too. We had a tupperware of rice with random things in it that my mom found in the never-ending junk drawer. I was to dig around in the rice and feel for the different things like a coin or pen cap or eraser and then pull it out. We would use the scrabble letters and playing cards to work my fingers and hand. My PT brought me an exercise ball and that thing alone had it own accessories like the ring that it sits in so it doesn't roll away and helps me keep my balance better. The pump that came with it was used to blow the ball and ring up. It even came with a patch kit. Lots of different balls; big ones to balance on, little ones to throw and mini ones to squeeze. I made sure to take a few of the instant ice and hot packs from rehab so that we could use them for various body parts as needed.

Another snag in the healing plans came along five months after my surgery. I spent the afternoon of my twenty-fifth birthday in the emergency room with my pregnant sister. I had been having some strange heart palpitations and racing off and on since a few weeks before but it was getting progressively frequent. At first I didn't think too much of it and had figured it had something to do with the opiates I was taking for pain. But it kept happening and I could find no rhyme or reason as to why it was happening and when it was happening. The morning of my birthday was like any other. I woke up and had some occupational therapy but we didn't do much because I wasn't feeling so good. I was jittery and my heart was racing a lot that day and I wasn't doing any physical activity that would induce that sort of thing. It was lasting longer and happening more frequently so I decided to call my family doctor to see what he suggested and he told me to go into the emergency room and have them check me out because this was something not to just ignore or ride out. I hung up the phone and told Mick what he said and I did not want to go anywhere because that night we were having a fun birthday dinner out with auntie and uncle and one of my good friends from college was going to join us too. So, I kept going about my business. Mick and I were hanging in the kitchen. I was on my computer signing up for an online dating service...lame I know, but I had told myself that if I didn't have a boyfriend or fiance or husband by my 25th birthday that I would just give the internet thing a short try. I paid for three months of service and started to complete the profile. It was extremely extensive and had many different types of questions from religious beliefs, occupation, location, etc. The typical questions, just a lot of them.

My favorite one was very straight up and important to me: how many kids you wanted. I knew my answer right away, 0, and was glad this was one of the questions that they would see the answer to because how upsetting would it be if you developed a relationship and connection with someone and then three months later find out they are on a different page with this serious subject of how many grandkids his parents wanted and how many babies he wanted to make. That subject might be taboo to ask about immediately (it could make you seem a bit crazy as you've barely established each other's likes and dislikes or how that other person likes their coffee) but for me, since I am 100% positive I could not handle being a mother I think that the other person should know that as soon as possible. I mean, I don't go around introducing myself as Angie, zero children please. On the other hand that is a huge part of a couple, whether or not they will be rearing some youngins, so for me it is hard to hold that back for very long. I don't want children because it could jeopardize my own health and I only weigh sixty pounds, most women gain half or more of me when they are pregnant, how would I carry a baby inside of me that weighs 10% of my weight? And then when the baby is born, how will I carry my baby? I can't even lift a half gallon of milk. I wouldn't be able to do any of the mothering duties, no diaper changing or putting the baby in the crib or carrying the baby around the house or pushing the carriage and so many more little things that aren't so little when you put them all together. That questionnaire made me feel like the money I was putting out to try this thing was somewhat worth it. I was hoping.

I had almost completed the dang thing, but my heart issues were feeling more intense and Mick and I decided to just go into the ER, we didn't want to take any chances. The closest one is five minutes away, but it is fairly new and has a horrible reputation. One story that gets around is that a local cop was shot and tried to get into the hospital doors but they were locked and the staff on the inside wouldn't let him in that way and told him to go to the ER. He was a COP and he was injured by a bullet. Some rules are meant to be broken, especially if it involves a dying cop. Yeah, so we went to this place. It was so weird, we just walked in and there wasn't really anyone there to direct the patients as to where they need to go or what to do. It was around lunchtime so the staff was pretty slim pickings. There was a large circular desk that looked like a nurses station so we walked up to it and just stood there for a couple of minutes, no one around. It felt like we weren't supposed to be there but it was an emergency room, aren't they supposed to be staffed 24/7?

Finally a nurse guy came up to us very un-urgently and casually asked us what's up and then brought us to a room right near the desk and had just a curtain separating us from the rest of the entire ER. He was in no rush and it was annoying that he wasn't showing too much concern as to why we were there. I thought emergency rooms meant they would immediately do a quick assessment to determine the status of your injury and then go from there. I had brought with us my typical packet of docs: medicines, current physicians, and surgeries. He started to ask the questions that pertained to those so I just gave them to him to add to my file. Oh man, he was becoming more and more obnoxious. He started by entering the medications into the system right there in front of us at a snail slow speed, pecking out each letter on the keyboard using only his pointer fingers. It felt like we were sitting there getting our toenails ripped off it was so agonizingly frustrating. Then he started spelling the medications wrong (even though the list I gave him was right in front of his eyes) and wasn't able to find them in the drop-down selection so he would have to start over and would fill the empty silence with very lame questions that ended up distracting him even more. The last straw for us was when he started to try and crack jokes, at my expense. Who does that? He would try and say something humorous about this medication or that patient he had and we just sat there looking at him not laughing at his lame jokes. I guess it's pretty slow in that ER so he tries to entertain himself any way that he can. When he was finally done entering this data he turned out not even to be the nurse! He went to go get someone to take my vitals while he watched and then put it in the chart. What an odd way to run an ER.

It only got stranger from that point. It turned out to feel like there goal was to see how many different people can see one patient in one visit. I ended up not even seeing the actual doctor until the very end of everything and it literally was for less than five minutes. It was so fast that I can't even remember what he looked like or how his demeanor was other than speedy to get out of there. The whole thing took a few hours and way longer than necessary. They had us waiting around long enough that I almost fell asleep on the examining table. Thank goodness for Mick being there to lighten the mood and entertain me. I had to go and get x-rays and the technician could barely speak English and wanted me to take my neck brace off so that he could get a better image. I explained over and over and in as many different ways I could that my brace had to stay on. Finally, he moved on from that and then put me in a wicked uncomfortable position with my arms up over my head (which I was not able to do at the time) and held it there for long enough to get the image he needed.

The doctor took forever to look at those and eventually came to talk to us for those few minutes. He said the x-rays looked okay but my heart rate was a bit higher than normal and he wanted me to wear a halter monitor for 24 hours. This contraption I had seen recently because one of my best friends had to wear one a few times because she was having heart troubles. The nurse put all these patch things all over my chest and ribs and then they all connected to this box that looked like a giant beeper that I had to wear hooked onto my pants. They were sticky little suckers and a few hairs definitely were removed when those things got pulled off, hair I didn't even know existed.

After we left the ER we rushed home to change into something more appropriate for dinner out (I guess sweats and huge t-shirts aren't normally acceptable wear outside of the home) and then went as quickly as I could to get out to the car and into the car and comfortable. It was a balancing act. We made it in time for our reservation and all seven of us were gathered around the round table and ready to have a nice meal together in celebration of my quarter-of-a-century-ness. The bread and oil was delivered and the wine poured. I know I was just in the ER an hour ago, but I only turn 25 once and get to celebrate out, so I had some wine! My plate of food was delivered and meat all cut up for me- another perk of not being able to use my right arm, I can't cut anything so it is done for me! We definitely enjoyed ourselves and I was very happy when they delivered me a piece of chocolate cake sans the singing crew. I get extremely embarrassed when the hostess and her staff come to the table and sing their rendition of the happy birthday song, even if it's not my birthday and/or if it's simply a table nearby. I get red in the face and feel my ears heating up just thinking about it. All in all, I had quite an adventurous and memorable birthday. I was able to go to sleep with a smile on my face despite the fact that I was hooked up to this heart monitor thing. That is what happens when you have great support from family and friends- no matter what the situation, it's bearable because of them.

The next day when I was able to take of the monitor we just had to drop it back off at the hospital. I didn't even have to go, dad just ran it over, easy as pie. They ended up sending the results to my family doctor and all was not normal but not anything to be extremely concerned about. The results were accurate, after some time the palpitations disappeared and I was feeling somewhat normal.

Next up was the lungs. I noticed a few days after the surgery that I would catch myself not breathing or trying to take a deep breath and not able to carry it through fully. I was hoping it was due to my neck brace. The trauma of the surgery was enough to do that as well. After the heart issues we wanted to make sure my respiratory system was in check because that is another issue that could come up with Morquio. Plus, almost all the medication I was taking could have an effect on that. My physical therapist recommended a pulmonary doctor in Lancaster. He knew him because it was his neighbor. That was good enough for me. We scheduled my first visit. It was nice only having to drive down town in

Lancaster instead of all the way to Baltimore of Philadelphia or Hershey. The office was at the hospital but in a building that was just completed. It was opposite of our typical specialist visits- the parking was not only easy to find but it was actually close to where we needed to be, well marked, and free. The oddest thing of all was that there were actual handicap spots available! That is a rarity. Anywhere. Next time you go to the mall take note not only of how many handicap spots there are and how many are taken but also of how few there are in comparison to how many other free-for-all spots there are. A very unbalanced ratio if you ask me. Especially since nowadays doctors give those placards out like candy. If you had a hurt pinky or ingrown toenail I bet you could get one. They should think of not only creating more spaces for those with the placards, but to categorize them so that those who truly need them will get to use them. Maybe divide it up by those who need a spot because they are in a wheelchair or are over the age of 75 or are obese.

Anyway, we got our prime spot and walked into the lobby which was so nice- tons of light coming in from the wall of windows, lots of open space, and not crowded or stinky. We followed the yellow brick road up to the elevator and off to the right was pulmonology. I completed the new patient paperwork and was called surprisingly fast back to the examining room. I was waiting for just a short time before my new doctor came in. I loved him immediately based on his choice of shoes. Before he even opened his mouth and exposed his accent I knew he had to be from somewhere other than the United States. You can always tell by the shoes. He was from somewhere in eastern Europe. He was great. Asked what he needed to know to figure out what was going on and quickly had a plan to discover my needs. He knew what he was doing even though he had never met me before and he had a confidence about him but what was even better was that there was not a hint of cockiness with that confidence, now that is unusual.

The next step was that I would go and do some tests and we would regroup and see what the results were. I went to the lab first and had to do some breathing into tubes and chambers with and without some sort of lung expander. Pulmonary Function Test. Who knows. But at that visit I do know what they did for sure, they took my ABG (arterial blood gas) which simply is a long needle plunged into my wrist to get blood directly from an artery. Sometimes (as in my case) it is difficult to find that artery and they have to do some digging with the needle. They have to find it by feeling around. My tech had to do it three times before she could get what she needed. Normally, this would hurt a lot, but this time since it was my right wrist that she got it from it was numb from nerve damage and it was just a slightly uncomfortable procedure. The worst part didn't come until later that day when it felt like my wrist had been stomped on. No bruising though! The point of that test was to analyze certain concentrations of different things- mainly to determine gas exchange levels in my blood related to my lung function.

The day before we left for Thanksgiving to go up to Massachusetts I had the second part of my testing- I had to do a sleep study to determine if I had sleep apnea. Great, now we have to test to make sure that I don't stop breathing in my sleep. I thought that the wires and stickies were bad when I had my heart test, well that was a walk in the park compared to this. The tech lady glued these things into my scalp and then taped other ones all over my body, literally. I did shave my legs and what I wore was simply an adult size t-shirt. I wanted to be as comfortable as possible. So she had me get ready for bed and I came out with that. No worries. It actually made it easier for me for when I had to pee. I didn't have to worry about getting the wires stuck in my pants and peeing on them or something like that. It took her about an hour to glue and tape everything where it needed to be. I even had to wear one of those oxygen things that go up the nose holes. That thing always makes me feel like a bull for some reason. Well, a bull with a ring in the nose. I was ready for battle once that was in!

The room I had to sleep in was very cozy and comfortable. At first when I saw it I immediately thought of rehab and I didn't know if I was going to be able to sleep very well there. That all changed once I sat on the bed. It was heavenly. There was a fabulous pillow-top mattress that made me feel like I was floating in the clouds. I got into bed and she needed to do some test runs to make sure that everything was hooked up properly. She left the room and all of the sudden she spoke and it was like God was talking to me! They had an intercom system hooked up so they could be in the control room and still communicate with the patient in the room. She had me close my eyes and do some breathing tests. When she was done she came back in quickly to my room to let me know we were all set to go. I was falling asleep during the tests so she knew I was tired and ready to go to bed. They monitored me all night and woke me up around the butt crack of dawn, 7am. It wasn't my lady friend though, it was a guy who was PERFECT for the morning shift to get me up. He had a very quiet and gentle spirit about him and I loved that. He came in and let me take as long as I needed to get up but he said first he has to do an ABG. I asked him why, since I had gotten one done a few weeks ago, it was procedure. I was able to lay in the cloud bed while he did it so it was better than the first time I had it done. It took him two needles to get it. Mission accomplished. Now all we had to do was get all those dang monitors off of me and unglue the many in my head that made me look like a martian. They even had a nice little breakfast cart for me to eat and drink something. They didn't know that I am not a breakfast person, but I ended up having a delicious banana that was too hard to open on my own so I had to ask for help. And I had a yummy hot black tea. My mom was coming to pick me up but was a bit later than we planned. So I just hung out and watched television in the room until she got there, I was just ready to get on the road to see family up North. It had been a very long time since we had celebrated a holiday up there.

9 ITALY REVISITED

Before I tried to go back to work full-time and wear myself down, I decided to take a month and spend it in Italy with Rose. I had plans to read, write, and paint while I was there. The GMAT was coming up quickly and I needed to study for that and couldn't seem to do it so easily at home with the baby as a distraction...playing with her is a lot more fun. Rose was coming home to visit at the end of July, so we planned that I would fly back with her and stay until mid-September.

08.18.10

Right now I am on the plane with Rose and Darcey waiting for everyone to board. We are going to Paris and then off we go to Florence. Lots of French, Italian, and smelly pits. We managed to get four seats in a row, but no first-class. I took my shoes off right away and put my socks on hoping for a comfortable flight. The captain just announced it will only take about six hours and 30 minutes to fly to the Charles de Gaulle airport. My eyes are very tired so maybe I will be able to sleep.

08.19.10

We've made it safe and sound. Rose and Giosué are out getting groceries and Darcey and I are just hanging around the apartment. The flights went quickly and easy. Pina is very sweet dog. I am glad she is around. The weather is warm and breezy. We arrived at 9:30 AM, dropped our bags off, and had breakfast outside. I think I will be taking over the guest room which needs a cleanup. We did some unpacking and took showers. I had to shave my legs in the bidet. Giosué took us to the center where we went to a restaurant called Montecielo. We had three different flavors of pizza: artichoke, buffalo mozzarella, and vegetarian. I had a piece of each. It was a Napoli-style pizzeria. Very neat atmosphere and architecture. The ceiling was vaulted and all brick. Of course we finished with a coffee and then had a gelato while walking around the center.

08.20.10

We took a bus into town (after we woke up past two in the afternoon) and stopped at a store where they make paper goods. I found an owl shaped bookmark and a book cover. Next we went to the Uffizi to see the Caravaggio exhibit and the ticket woman told us that I was able to get in free of charge to any public Museum as well as whoever was pushing me. So now I should be admitted at no cost to places like the Bargello, Boboli gardens, the Academia, etc. We left just as they were closing. Rose made pasta with spinach and tomatoes for dinner. Darcey and I cleaned the kitchen up, played Scrabble, and looked at pictures while Rose and Giosué took a walk. We finally got hooked up to the Internet and we were able to talk with Mick and Gia... perfect ending to the day.

08.21.10

Today we took a drive to a lake. We went to the store around the corner (Co Op) and bought things for a picnic lunch. We packed our food, paints, pencils, books, and Pina and off we went into the countryside. Lots of windy roads later we pulled off into the middle of nowhere onto some sort of campground field and had a picnic. Pina puked. Rose and Giosué ' wanted to take a nap, but I just wanted to get to the lake. When we finally got there we set out our towels on the rocks, no sand. We went in the water for a bit and when I got out I laid down and fell asleep. I woke up with rock indents all over my body. Thankfully, we took the Autostrada back into the city and it only took a half hour. Rose cooked dinner-baked chicken, potatoes, and zucchini. After dinner we took a walk for a half hour to get gelato. Good thing it was open, most places were still on holiday and not open yet. The weather was perfect to take a walk and it was very peaceful and quiet.

08.22.10

It is Sunday. Giosué took us to a Nazarene church. I discovered I should not be eating gelato because this morning I was so sick and I thought I was going to throw up in the car on the way to church. I made it there but had to go straight to the restroom and then stayed there for a half hour and missed most of their worship. The service was in Italian and I could catch things here and there mainly because I had already developed an understanding of the topic from before. At some point it took all I had to stay awake and the heat was no help. Everyone wanted to talk with Giosué after so it took a long time to get out of there. Somehow we ended up dropping this kid off that we didn't know. He was from

Albania and spoke no English and horrible Italian. When we finally got home we had a pasta salad lunch and took long naps. Later in the evening Giosué drove us near the center to park the car and we walked to get a coffee. We were able to find a table outside to enjoy the evening and all the people walking around. It was nice and warm to have drinks outside, it felt like we were in a movie it was so perfect. We continued to walk around the city and had plans to go to a pizza place but when we arrived it was closed (for the holiday). We saw some weird things that night. There was a girl with a miniskirt on and knee-high boots that were furry and made her look like Chewbacca. Then we found a car that was burnt and melted to a crisp on the side of the road. We were walking by some shops looking through the windows at their decorations and there was one where it looks like a naked man was laying on a table with only a mask on. Of course it was a mannequin, but the way it was set up made you do a double take. Ironically, it was a clothing store. We ended up driving to a place called Pizza Man and ate dinner at 9:30 PM. Pina was with us and they let us have her in the restaurant with us. Rose told me last time they had eaten there Pina had tried to bite the waiter. After dinner we went home and hung out. Mick and Gia were online for us to talk to.

08.23.10

Darcey and I went to the local market and grocery store in the morning. It was just two blocks from Rose's apartment. On our way there some old guy threw breadcrumbs out his window right as we were below him. Later we found out he does that to Rose too, he must lead an exciting life. The little market was pretty pathetic. Nothing good and very disorganized. There was one stand that only sold crappy yarn and another stand that had cheap clothing that looked like it would fall apart after one wear. There were some vegetables but those looked unpromising as well. The grocery store we went to next was nothing special either. I bought a plant for the room we were staying in (also now known as my room). We also bought snacks for when we play Scrabble and some beers because they were cheaper than water.

On our way home we somehow went the wrong way and it took us at least an hour to get back on the right path. Luckily, we weren't too lost because we didn't know Rose's street name or phone number and we spoke no Italian and in that neighborhood they were all old people who don't speak English. When we finally were back at the apartment we had lunch. Delicious tomato and mozzarella, fresh as can be.

Darcey and I took bus 17 to the piazza San Marco. The first bus driver would not let us on. I think we were taking too long to get on the bus for him and he wasn't sure if we wanted to ride. Once we found our way to the center we wandered through the market searching for treasures. I found a nice scarf for only two euros. Sales guys are super annoying with their calling out and dumb questions to try and get you to look at their crap. They would ask where we were from and then tell us they had a cousin near there or would tell us how beautiful we were and that their jewelry which make us even more beautiful. Lame. I guess it works enough that they try it on everyone. They just want to make money any way they can. We were over the market but still had time to kill before we met up with Rose and Giosué. We sat outside at a bar and had drinks. We wandered around some more.

Finally, it was soon time to meet up with them so we went back to piazza San Marco. There were benches surrounding the statue that we sat at and people watched. Next to us there were two old guys having an intense conversation using their hands to talk. One lady nearest to us had two little white dogs. The lady seemed not all there. The last person we watched was this cute, fat little Asian boy. When Rose and Giosué picked us up we drove to the piazzale Michaelangelo. It was here that we were able to watch the sun set over the entire city. There were stairs that overlooked the river that we sat on to eat cheese and bread and drink wine from plastic cups. It was so beautiful that it seemed fake like the postcards that are bought at museums. After we got back we went to get gelato and I picked strawberry with no milk. Let's hope my stomach is okay with that.

08.24.10

We started our day at the Bargello. My favorite. I still can't believe it used to be a prison and where people were executed. We got in free and skipped the line. We looked around for about an hour which made us work up an appetite. After seeing all of that, we stopped for lunch at a cute little café down the street. I had spaghetti, salad, and an espresso. A bunch of Americans were seated next to us and had ordered beverages and the waiter was taking too long (according to them) so they just got up and left without paying for their drinks and service. How rude. Once we were finished our meal we did some shopping. First, we went to a jewelry store and I bought two pairs of earrings. Next, we went on a shoe hunt for Darcey. A few stores later we found them. We walked towards the Boboli gardens and Rose was telling us that she did not like walking in this area because

Marco's dad had a stand there and sometimes Marco works for him. This was the last person on earth that we wanted to see. Just when she finished telling me this she saw him sitting only about 20 feet away. She just booked it out of there as fast as she could push my wheelchair on the uneven cobblestone without popping me out. She didn't think he saw us. We walked over the famous bridge that sells all the jewelry you could ever imagine. Up the steep entrance to the Pitti Palace we went to get free tickets to get into Boboli gardens. We had to walk up an even steeper hill when we are inside the grounds. And what made it worse was the fact that it was gravel not a smooth pathway. At one point I had to get out of my chair and Rose carried me up the rest of the way while Darcey pushed my empty wheelchair. We stopped in a grassy area, put down a blanket, I wrote while Rose and Darcey drew. It was nice. There were a lot of French people walking by our blanket. One young Italian couple was sitting on the grass near us and the boy came over to ask us if we had any bug spray. I guess he didn't see the huge welts Rose and Darcey had all over their arms and legs.

We only saw two cats there and no mice so I guess that was a good thing. We didn't attempt to push me in my wheelchair down the hill, I could just picture myself rolling down on the ground if we did that. So once again, Rose carried me and Darcey took the wheelchair. It is a good thing that it only weighs about ten pounds! This worked up an appetite in us all so before leaving the Center we had to get gelato. I had the chocolate with hazelnut. The place we had it at had a bunch of wine bottles with the name Angelini. I never knew there was a wine named after me.

08.25.10

This morning Darcey and I took the 17 bus again to San Marco. We felt a lot more at ease taking the bus this time now that we knew where we were going and where our stop was. First we had to stop at the bar right near the bus stop to start our day off right with an espresso. Across the street was what used to be a cloister but now is a museum. We went inside and got our free tickets. This was one of the museums on my list of "to see" so I was very excited. I really enjoyed the style of the paintings and there was one room that had all the info on the scripts and ink making and how they used wood as canvases. We had to find a guard to actually take us to this room because there was only one way opened for the public and that required going up several flights of stairs. He took us around some back entrance and through a courtyard with construction being done. There was an elevator on the outside of the building that he put me in and up we went.

We were on a time constraint and planned with Rose to have lunch back at her apartment. We decided to go to the Academia to see David. Once again we were able to skip the lines but this time it actually made a huge difference because people were lined up literally down the block to get in. When we went in it was pretty packed. Lots of large groups of tourists. Next on our to-do list was to get tshirts for Darcey's brothers. We headed on down to the markets. While we were there I picked up a watch, sunglasses, and a leather bracelet. We got back on the bus and were not sure of our stop and ended up getting off too soon. There was one of those street corner news stands where Darcey asked for directions and off we went. We were not too far off (just one stop too early), so that was good. We had perfect timing though because right as we were approaching Rose's apartment building Rose was getting back from the grocery store with stuff to make lunch. We had planned the night before to go up to Feasole in the afternoon, but we ended up not going there. Rose started organizing and moving stuff around in her apartment and wasn't finished until 5 PM. Instead we took a bus up to some small town that had a countryside lookout of the city. It was a scary bus ride. The walls were so close to the bus I thought we really were going to crash or roll off the edge of the road down some huge mountain. We got off at the town's main square. It was like a ghost town. There were maybe five stores there and only one open. Even the church looked all closed up. We wandered around and found some amazing views. I was afraid to take the bus back down, but I was even more nervous to miss the last bus back into Florence. We didn't stay up there very long, but definitely long enough. When we made it safely back down Rose made risotto and then she went with Giosué to work (to clean a gym) because she wanted to spend time with him. Darcey and I hung out, played scrabble and checked out the train schedule to Viareggio- the beach that is less than two hours away by train. We went to bed around midnight with intentions of getting up early and catching the 9 AM train to the beach.

08.26.10

We didn't make the 9 AM train, not a big surprise. We made the 10 AM with only a few minutes to spare. We ended up packing a lunch and we ate on the beach. The train ride was very comfortable and did not seem long at all. It wasn't too busy and we were able to find seats next to each other. When we got off the train we only had to walk a few blocks to get to the actual beach.

We were seeing the Mediterranean Sea! We rented two beach chairs and an umbrella for fifteen euros. Right away Rose and I went in the ocean. Mainly, because I had to pee and that was the only way I was going to be able to go. It was amazing. The waves weren't overpowering and the water was shallow. When I got out I lathered up with sunscreen. I did not want sun poisoning or burn to ruin my trip! I took a nice nap while they went in for some time. I went once more into the ocean and then hung out for the rest of the time in the sun. My goal was accomplished- a tan and no burn! The other two ding dongs did get a bit of a burn.

We took the 16h30 train but almost missed it because my credit card was blocked by my bank for suspicious activity (even though I had called them prior to leaving the States to let them know I would be using it outside of the country). And then there were the stairs. The elevator that we needed to take to get to the platform where our train was picking us up was out of service and we had to run down and then up two flights of stairs with our bags and almost no time left. We made it and could relax for the trip back, as much as one can relax with a few extra pounds of sand all up in the bathing suit and in the hair.

When we got back we took showers, got ready, and went out to dinner at a pizzeria around the corner from Rose's apartment. It was so nice out and we were able to eat outside on their patio in the back. It was Darcey's last dinner here with us. Her flight was early the next day. We had pizzas and coffee and just enjoyed being there in the moment and taking our time. We were planning on having gelato with a few of Rose's friends from church and Giosué was going to meet us there after he was finished with work. On the way to the gelateria we stopped to get Pina and walked there. We met three of Rose's friends. One was very handsome and funny. He could be my husband, but the only way that would happen would be if he wanted his green card. We shall see, I am not opposed to it. The other two were a couple and the girl didn't know too much English, but she was very sweet and a good sport about us all talking in English. I am sure that it was frustrating. At the end of the night Rose made sure to speak in Italian so she could feel more included. We were there so long we actually got kicked out of the place. Closing time. So we stood outside for another hour just chatting. When we got back Darcey had to pack and then we skyped with Mom, Mick, and Gia. They were showing us the progress of the kitchen renovations. It will be exciting to go home to a brand new kitchen. Bedtime rolled in around three in the morning. Rose and Giosué stayed up even longer talking in the kitchen about who-knows-what. I was sad to be losing my travel buddy and roommate.

08.27.10

It was a very mellow, productive day. Since Darcey had a flight to catch we got up early and got ready and headed to the bar for one last coffee and pastry together. I couldn't eat anything and I had an espresso just to make sure I got my caffeine kick before I started feeling my withdrawal symptoms. We paid the sitting fee and enjoyed ourselves. When Darcey left to catch her bus to the airport Rose went off to teach an English lesson. I was able to stay at the apartment and hung around with Pina. I rearranged and organized and then tried to paint. I haven't painted since my surgery and I figured I might as well try with my new dominant, left hand. That did not go well and so I resorted to studying for the GMAT. When

Rose came home she made a delicious salad with tuna on it and fresh olive oil that is nowhere to be found in the U.S.

My future husband came after lunch to get help from Rose because he had to take an English language proficiency test later that week as a requirement for a school he wanted to get into...in the United States. See? It was already happening that we would eventually be in the same country again. I sat in the kitchen with them because I was curious to see what this exam entailed and I wanted to see how his English was. Well, let's just say I don't think I would be able to pass this exam. It's all about speed and accuracy and showing the spectrum of the language. Giosué came to pick Rose up to go to a wedding he was taking video of for a few hours. It seemed like I had been alone for an eternity by the time they did get home. Rose had prepared dinner for us three- a stir fry with bean noodles that she brought from the States.

08.28.10

There was a public pool nearby that we took a walk to in the afternoon. It wasn't so hot out which made it less appealing to go, but I wanted to get out of the house and to go somewhere different. We thought we were going to have to pay to get in, but they waived the fee for us because I was in my wheelchair. Score! We entered and unloaded all our crap. We jumped in and the water was way too freezing for my nerves so I just sat on the side of the pool with my feet in the water. There were a bunch of obnoxious kids all around that were jumping and splashing us. It's not like we could get mad at them, we were at a public pool and they did pay to enjoy themselves. I noticed as we were trying to sun bathe with clouds in the sky that everyone had a swim cap on. I pointed that out to Rose and questioned if we were required to wear one. She didn't think so, but on our way out of there we did end up seeing a sign that was put up in the past few weeks announcing that it was a new rule. Whoopsies. Well, I guess it was not a rule they felt comfortable to enforce with a girl in a wheelchair, otherwise I feel like they would have mentioned it to us when we got there. We only stayed for about an hour, not even long enough to dry off. It wasn't warm enough out.

We stopped at our favorite bar near Rose's apartment and had a coffee on our way back. There was an old lady in there hanging out and she loved me. She called me her little treasure. I love old people for that. They always seem to love me, no matter how funky I look. They have lived their lives and know what really matters and is worth investing in. Now if I could only find that mentality in a guy my age. Well, that and also that he would be attracted to me.

My little miss Betty Crocker went to the grocery store to get some things for dinner. She ended up making a yummy pasta dish and for dessert she made tiramisu! It was delicious. After I had gone to bed for the night the wind decided to pick up and was so strong that all the doors and windows to the entire building were slamming shut and open. It woke me up and scared the crap out of me. I had to get up to grab my journal off the porch because I thought it was going to blow away. I had a hard time falling back to sleep and staying asleep. We weren't planning on going to church tomorrow morning so at least I didn't have to worry about getting up and ready.

08.29.10

Rose and I had a nice coffee out on the terrace together this morning. The weather has remained beautiful despite the wind storm last night. It makes my heart happy to have sunshine around this much. I love being able to keep the windows wide open and without a screen. No need to worry about stink bugs! No insects to keep out except for mosquitoes. Rose made a delicious french toast with peaches for lunch. Giosué came over and spent some time here and then headed off to catch his flight to Sardina to visit with his cousin for five days. Rose was upset about that because she wouldn't be able to see him. I can't sympathize with her, I never had a boyfriend to love, let alone a boyfriend who went away for a week. I finally started my book. I decided it will be about my last surgery and the recovery period and experiences. I wanted to stop a few times but managed to push myself through and came up with a rough, basic outline. Now I have to fill it in between. I figure when Rose has to go and give lessons I can stay home and work on my book step by step.

In the late afternoon Rose and I went to Zara. I bought some very nice, age appropriate dresses, sweaters, and a pair of shorts. Jackpot for me! We had to stop at Rose's job on the way home to pick up some lesson plans and then we decided to walk home the rest of the way because there was a game at the studio near her apartment and a lot of the surrounding roads were shut down to vehicles. There were a ton of fans dressed in purple gear and a lots of riot police on hand. All of the news crews and their vans surrounded the stadium. You could feel the electricity in the air. Fans were heard until late in the night blaring their horns and yelling who knows what to each other after a successful win. Before we went to bed we were able to skype with Darcey and talk to her for an hour. It made me miss her more.

08.30.10

Well the morning started out with a sunny sky and some clouds, but by mid-afternoon we had ourselves a storm. This was only a bummer for me because my terrace sitting plans were out of the question. I had to resort to the kitchen and my room. I studied for the GMAT and read a book. Since studying leads me to napping I found myself waking up to the winds and crashing windows. Rose was cleaning the house. I woke up and was in the bathroom when a glass-breaking sounded. It ended up being a lamp and glass of water on the desk in my room that got blown over. I thought I had closed my windows but I guess not tight enough. It rained for a few hours and then cleared up but was so chilly. At least cold for what I had been experiencing the past couple of weeks here. We ended up making an outing to the grocery store and got some stuff to make a potato soup. Good food for this type of weather. Since it was such a blasé day for us it was nice to be able to connect to Gia on skype later in the evening and make her laugh all the way across the world. Mick gave us a tour of the kitchen and the progress they are making. It looks like a mess and is totally torn apart. I am very happy to not be involved or around for that whole project, talk about stressful. A house without a kitchen seems to be a problem producer.

08.31.10

It was an eventful day today. The rain stayed away and the warm breezes were blowing on in. Rose had a lesson in the morning but when she got home from that we started our day together. She made me a cappuccino before she left which was delicious as usual. My stomach doesn't seem to be enjoying the milk that is in it though so I spent the rest of the time she was away in the bathroom. It wasn't too bad because the window is right by the toilet so I can get fresh air and watch the clouds while sitting on the pot. We picked up the bus across the street after and headed to a dollar store. And I thought the dollar stores in the U.S. are random, here it is so odd and all jammed into such a tiny store. It's like a treasure chest and everywhere you look is something interesting and nothing you'd expect. We got some things like a toilet plunger and some wine glasses.

On our way back to the apartment we stopped at a shoe store and a clothing store. No shoes but I did get a jacket thing. We walked around and stopped to have an espresso. Of course the bar tender/coffee man was handsome. We grabbed the bus back but jumped off a few stops before our typical stop so that we could just walk and enjoy the sunshine, make up for the lack of vitamin D from yesterday. We arrived back at the house sweaty and hungry so Rose made some lunch. I studied (napped) while Rose continued to clean and organize and get things all ready for her new roommate.

We made plans to have dinner with one of Rose's friends that was in town for a few weeks that she knew from her college days in Baltimore. She said that he is a painter. We took the bus in to meet him at piazza San Marco and as we were waiting for him she told me about him. She said he had made his own frames (glasses) out of wood and how he had to go to different lens places and try to convince them to make lens for his frames and he actually got one of them to do it and he now wore these things. I immediately was thinking that this guy was going to be one of her really off the wall art school friends and that he was going to be looking like Woody Allen. She proved me wrong on several occasions about having bizarre art friends, but there were enough times that they really were weird, so I just planned on having an interesting dinner with a guy that makes his own wooden frames. I am looking all around us for a guy that is out of place but don't find one. Instead comes a normal looking American with his cargo shorts and worn-looking tee. And then there were his flip-flops. I don't know of many Italians that would actually wear flip-flops in public unless they are at a beach so I figured he was our guy. I could breathe a sigh of relief that he didn't have his home-made specs on. The moment he spoke with his Jersey accent I knew we were going to get along just fine. We hadn't planned where we were going to eat ahead of time, so we picked a Mexican joint. He was familiar with the place and said they were cheap and tasty. They had outside seating so I didn't care about anything and was happy just to be outside. We were sitting near these grubby-looking dudes with unkempt beards and weird vibes. The one was blind and was smoking a pack of cigarettes which he finished and then moved on to those little cigar things. They had many visitors and seemed to be very popular with the folks around. It was one of those types of restaurants that made you feel cool because you selected one that the locals go to frequently and it seems like they slipped up by attracting you and letting you sit and dine there. I would rather pretend to fit in and eat at places like that then to go to some ritz-y place where you pay an arm and a leg but are treated as tourists. They don't even bother speaking their language to you and it always makes me feel disappointed that they could spot my american-ness. Anyway, we ordered some nachos for a starter. My stomach wasn't feelin' food that night so I grazed, but it didn't help that the table was so high I could barely reach the plate and there were no napkins so I didn't want to be eating and have a mess that I wouldn't have been able to clean. I didn't know this guy so I didn't want to seem like a total weirdo. Next up we ordered some veggie burritos and I had only a few bites. The benefits of eating with a boy included finishing off whatever I didn't eat and he paid for it all. We had some sangria and coffee to top it all off and sat there talking for hours. It was good conversation and we all had a very enjoyable evening in beautiful Italy. Why does everything seem better in a foreign country, even the simple things like dining out or walking the city? Adam walked us back to the bus station and we agreed to get together again before he left. Rose and I made it home around midnight. I read a bit and then fell right asleep with the window open and all.

09.01.10

I can't believe it's already September. I love this month, it is the best weather of the year and new starts for everyone. It's even better when I don't have to work and am able to spend most of it in Italy with my sister. It feels surreal that I can just be alive and thriving and having such a great time doing pretty much nothing. Other than it being the first of the month, nothing crazy happened today. Rose just had lessons until noon. She made pasta for lunch. I painted, studied, and read all day. Once again the weather was marvelous and I was able to continue enjoying the terrace- in my pajamas. I know a few of the neighbors can probably see, but too bad, I do what I want. In the afternoon we decided to go to the dog park nearby. Of course on our way we had to stop and get some gelato. I wanted to be able to enjoy it, but I was unable to get past what my repercussions would be the next day if I ate a lot of it. I chose hazelnut flavor and there was an entire nut in it. Delicious. There were a bunch of dogs when we arrived at the park. We went through the gate unnoticed and walked to the back of the lot where they were all hanging out together. The owners were playing cards and sitting and chatting together while their dogs ran around together and chased one another. Pina didn't seem to want to join in at first, but Rose started to run around and she had a following after her so Pina got involved. I took some pictures of it all. There was one little dog that seemed to be intimidated by my wheelchair and would bark at me. Another one came up to the wheel, sniffed it, and pissed right on it! I couldn't do anything but laugh, he was just claiming my wheel. One of the owners came over and grabbed the dog and apologized. No big deal, how often can you say a dog peed on you? There was one beagle that got really into chasing Pina around. They were fun to watch, especially since Pina was a bigger dog.

Rose made us cous cous and zucchini for dinner. I love love love cous cous. It reminds me of when I lived in France and would eat that all the time because it was one of the only things I could make in my tiny apartment kitchen.

09.02.10

Rose and I went to SACI today so she could work on some of her sculptures. While she did that, I was, once again, studying for the GMAT. I also painted for a nice chunk of time. I only had fizzy water, so I used that with my gauche. It worked. It was frustrating painting with my left hand. An unpleasant reminder of the bad things that have happened because of my surgery. But the good tends to win and I realized that I was sitting in Italy painting a beautiful winding staircase that was covered in ivy. Something seen only in a fairy tale. It is amazing the things that can counteract my negative thoughts. My heart can go from sinking and discouraged feeling to completely opposite-soaring and untouchable. I live in the moment and am grateful I am able to do so. Instead of dwelling on the horrible changes that have occurred in my life within the past fourteen months, I am able to appreciate the fact that I am sitting in a garden with the sun warming me inside and out in a country whose language I can't even speak. Who cares that I no longer can write with my right hand or that I have a hard time shaving my armpits? What does it matter that I need to use a wheelchair to get around? I can take that kind of thinking and turn it around into what I am blessed with. I pray that I will always be able to do that. Awareness of the present is something that's kept me from staying in those dark places that are so easily fallen into. Moving forward and onward no matter what.

We bought sandwiches on our way to the studio. Rose and I have eaten from there before, it a nice place tucked in behind one of the many stands in the street markets. Not too many tourists walk on the backsides of the carts, so it is easier to get through to places. The woman who works there knows Rose from going so frequently; the ceramics instructor that Rose teaches with took her to this place and they've been going there ever since.

When she was finished working on her pieces she had a lesson to teach. We had salads for dinner. I got all of my stuff ready for the beach. I finished my book. Rose was organizing and cleaning out her desk, we were finding some interesting things. She had kept a list of my quotes from the last time I was visiting them in Italy, that brought back some fun memories.

09.03.10

In honor of dad's birthday we had a beach day. We were able to jump on the 10 am train to Viareggio. This time around we had Adam come with us. Rose packed a lunch for us and we stopped at the corner bar to start our day out right with a quick coffee before we caught the bus to the train station. We thought we were going to miss the train because we were cutting it so close. Rose was able to send Adam a text to buy our train tickets because he was already there waiting for us. So we jumped off the bus and jumped onto the train. We chatted the whole ride there which was entertaining and made it go by super fast. The people around us were probably annoyed to have three young people talking in English for two hours near them. We tried to keep our voices as low as possible, but sometimes that is hard when you're having a good time. Once we arrived at our stop we only had to walk a few blocks until we were at the actual beach. Sand on the ground, smell of ocean nearby, umbrellas as far as the eyes can see, and beautiful mountains in the distance.

Before we settled down we stopped to get a pastry and some coffee We had be discussing bread on the train for some reason and it made me hungry, but not yet ready for lunch so we had a snickity-snack. I chose one with chocolate and once again was not surprisingly unable to finish it. Luckily, we had our left-overs finisher, Adam. We didn't have to twist his arm too hard to get him to eat it. I just gave him the ultimatum of his mouth or the trash, that one seems to work usually. It's hard for some people to see things go into the trash. Once on the beach we had to rent two chairs and umbrellas and stashed my wheelchair at the beach house place. Rose gave me a lift down the wooden walk way and onto the sand to our assigned spots. It wasn't too far from the water, but not as close as we were used to getting when we were in New Jersey.

It was a great beach day. The weather was warm and sunny. There was not a cloud in the sky so we were able to see the Carrera mountains off on the skyline. We got into the water right away but this time I wasn't able to stay in as long as I wanted to. The water had a chill to it and my whole body seemed to be stiffening up and spasming and it got to the point where my right arm was bent and wouldn't straighten out and my hips were chattering in their non-existent sockets. I had Rose carry me out and plopped me on my towel to warm up and de-cramp. Thankfully, it didn't take but a few minutes because the sand was so warm. Like a giant warming blanket. I thought it was going to make me fall asleep but it turned out that some old guy nearby and his extremely loud snores kept me from drifting off. Every now and then he would snort and all I could do was laugh. People probably thought I was crazy, some girl laying on her towel laughing at herself with no one around.

At one point these teenage boys came a bit too close to comfort when Rose and Adam were still in the water. I had to get up and move to a beach chair so they wouldn't squash me. They seemed to think it was the perfect place to wrestle each other. It was not just two boys either, they were large and obnoxious and all three were rolling around with one another and coming onto our towels. By the time they were done messing around Rose's towel was half covered in sand. Eventually they stopped and only then did Rose and Adam return. Oh well.

We sat around and ate our lunch that Rose prepared for us, tuna sandwiches which ironically both Adam and I neither liked usually. She made them deliciously though, she has a way of making things I normally don't care for into something decently tasty. We drank our wicked sweet peach tea that made me feel sick, but I drank it anyway because of it being nice and ice cold-literally, we had put them in the freezer the night before.

We decided to catch the 16h30 train and once again almost missed it thanks to the non functioning elevators. We were stupid enough to expect that they would be working this time around. Rose wanted to get back to the apartment to cook because Giosué and his cousin were arriving tonight from their week-long vacation in Sardina. It was rush hour when we got back to the train station in Florence. We grabbed the bus and it took an hour for them to arrive at our stop. At one point the ticket-checker dude (technical title, huh?) came on the bus. A girl got caught without purchasing a ticket and tried to play it off like she had no clue and didn't get what was going on. She was fined, kick off the bus, and stared at by all. It was enough to make me want to buy a ticket and I wasn't even required to. Of course I didn't actually buy one, but it made me scared not to have a ticket. One of Rose's old roommates never bought bus passes and would always risk the fine because it was worth it to him to take the fine and pay it than to just buy tickets.

We got back to the apartment and tried to take the elevator up to Rose's floor but it wasn't working. It was a few flights of stairs and she had to carry all of our bags and me on her back. Once the door was opened we figured something was wrong, it was pitch black and normally there is some sort of light coming from all the other apartments around hers shining in from the terrace. She found out the electricity was cut off for some reason. The street light on the front of her building was working so that gave us a bit of light in the bathroom and bedrooms, but it was super dark in the kitchen. Rose busted out all of her candles and put them up all over. Since she has a gas stove she was able to finish the dinner. In the meantime, the boys were off at the store getting some beverages to have with dinner. Rose made chicken soup and a salad. It was hard to converse with them. Giosué's cousin, Mino, did not speak English. It was the first time Rose had met him, so they were naturally speaking in Italian. The first hour was okay and I was able to follow the jist of the conversation. But my brain began to give out and I couldn't concentrate on it anymore. I just let my mind wander and ate my food. Occasionally Rose would remember to translate for me, but for the most part I was on my own. Whatever, I was in Italy after all. Half way through our meal the electricity came back on and all the lights were so bright after being in candle light for a couple of hours. After dinner they wanted to go and get some gelato and I had had a long enough day and wasn't up for that so I stayed home and went to bed.

09.04.10

Oh what a long day it was, and I thought yesterday evening's dinner was challenging. It is very difficult to be with people that only speak a language you don't understand. I had to be in my head a lot today, just entertaining myself. I would try to listen and figure out what the conversation involved, but my language brain cells exhausted themselves pretty quickly. It began a bit before noon when the boy and his cousin came to Rose's apartment to pick us up. Apparently we were going on a hunt for new frames for Giosué. This didn't sound too bad, a guy who needs new glasses, they aren't picky when it comes to that, right? I'll answer that so there are no questions, no, it is not simple. This was one of those instances where it is not helpful to assume or stereotype, here I had it in my head that he is a guy and therefore does not take a million years to shop for himself, not true.

Rose and I figured we would go to a lens store and pick out a pair and then move on to the more important things, like lunch. I guess Mino is his personal stylist because those two had to get opinions from one another one each and every frame. We spent about 45 minutes in the first store, some place we had to drive to and go over the river and all around to get to. They went crazy trying on every pair. They would just talk to each other, Rose would occasionally give a thumbs up or down, but I literally just sat there in my wheelchair invisible to them.

No one cared what I thought or anything. All Italian to each other and me trying to figure out what they were saying about the glasses and wondering how one could have so much to say on that topic. Glasses are glasses, no? No. After the first store I thought I heard we were going to put the search on hold and go for lunch. I didn't open my mouth to say anything, I was so thirsty and had cotton mouth so I don't think my mouth could open even if I wanted to. We got back in the car and headed to the city. I think we drove around for an hour trying to find a parking spot near the train station. We drove around one block four times and at a pace that we could have walked faster than. Traffic was horrendous. I started to feel sick.

Rose must have noticed I was turning pale and shriveling up into nothing. She told Giosué to just find a parking already. I just wanted to drink some water, I felt like I had been in the tundra all day. My medicines do that to me, and those side effects seem to become stronger when I take them on an empty stomach, which I did that morning. I was searching the streets as we drove around for those people like in Baltimore that sell the newspaper to you in the car, hoping they would have only water to sell. No luck.

We finally went down a street that looked like it was residential/permit parking and decided to park there anyway. It was around two in the afternoon by this point. There was a specific restaurant that Giosué was taking us to. We were walking through the city and crowds and obnoxious tourists. The worst part was going by all these open food places and not stopping. I would have eaten kebab by that point. We turned the corner of a quieter street and the place is closed for holiday. Unbelievable, but not. Now it was Rose's turn to take us to a place to stop and eat at, but her choice was closed as well. Now it was getting to the time where the deli's and sandwich shops were no longer making food so we had to go to a place that catered to tourists. Rose convinced them to stop wandering around and just sit down at a table. We did and you could cut the tension with a knife. I was so hungry I didn't feel hungry anymore. I couldn't and didn't want to talk because of my dry mouth and thirst like no other. My back and butt were drenched in sweat from the heat and the fact that my wheelchair cushions are black. I had to pee and Rose went with me leaving the guys to order. When we got back to the table we had water. I drank an entire liter. My veggie pizza was nothing special, they were pretty charred. The talk continued in Italian and I just concentrated on filling my face with water and food. To end the meal we did get coffee, thank God. I needed something to wake me up. After our recharge the search for glasses continued. I felt like I was in that movie Ground Hog Day, I have a lot of hate for that movie. I can't stand repeating things over and over (movies that is)- once and done is enough for me... let's get to the point and move on from there. Not today. We went to the same stores just in different locations. About six of them. I convinced Rose to take me away from them for a moment to go to the bathroom again and get more water and take some drugs. I was sore from just sitting in my chair. I was ready to be done. The last one we went into there was a very rico-suave type of guy trying to help them. I guess he was pretty entertained by it all. In the end, four hours later, nothing was purchased. It was gelato time. I was already nauseous and not in the mood to hang around and chit chat. But we did. We sat right on one of the bridges over the Arno. From there we headed back to the car, so I thought. Since I was no longer trying to understand what they were talking about in Italian I had no clue what their plans were. For some reason we stopped in this high-end furniture shop called Flair. There was a lot of beautiful pieces in there, but so expensive. There were three stairs up into the store and we got up no problem. Giosué was pushing me and I was so nervous he was going to bump into and/or break something. We end up near the stairs and I started to feel anxious that I was going to be falling out of my chair and down the stairs. I didn't want to say anything, but Giosué ended up getting too close and it started to tip down the stair. He caught the chair in time and I am pretty sure it scared him more than me, at least I saw it coming and had prepared myself. He let Rose take over the pushing duty. I hate when that happens, we are out somewhere and one person is pushing my wheelchair and then get tired and the chore gets passed on to someone else to suffer through. I can feel it in the way they move and push. I can feel the banging on the handle bars and hear the huffing and sense the dread of dealing with the chair. I can't do anything about it. I try to ignore it.

A few stores later and a few hours longer we finally arrived back to the car, it wasn't towed. The last stop was so torture-some. It was a disorganized clothing store with piles of unfolded jackets and pants and shirts in huge bins. You have to dig through them to find not only the style you want but also the size. The boys were trying on these military type coats. At least Mino actually bought one, so it wasn't in vain. It was getting dark as we were leaving to get back to Rose's apartment. I just wanted to change out of my clothes and put my sweatpants on. Those things always make you feel better. I couldn't wait to stretch out and lay flat on my stomach on my bed. Sitting all day in that wheelchair can take a toll. When my head hit my pillow that night I passed out.

09.05.10

Giosué came to pick us up at 9 AM to go to church. He had to be there early to set up the camera and all that other technical stuff. The church rents a room in a movie theater. There is a bar on the first floor that is open on Sundays so that is where Rose and I went to hang out until the service began. We were immediately greeted by an old gentleman and he was asking Rose how she was and all the general questions. He then pinched my check, which normally would bother me, but since he was over the age of 70, he had a pass. The head patting and cheek squeezing are a definite no-no when it comes to me, of course unless you're old. Same with calling me cute. Just don't do it. So we ordered our coffee and pastries and sat at the tables there with the other random people reading the newspaper or chit chatting with their friends. The surprising thing about this building was that it was truly accessible for wheelchairs. To get to the place where the church held the service we had to go up a few flights of stairs. I immediately saw the bars that indicate a powerlift/elevator for a chair. And then down comes Giosué riding the beastly thing that goes as slow as a snail. It was quite amusing to see him standing on the platform. It took him a bit of time to arrive and they loaded me up and walked next to me as it climbed the stairs. I was glad there was no one around to watch this.

Not many people came because of it still being what the Italians call their holiday (a month long-how nice!). As one of the pastors spoke I struggled to keep my eyes open. My eyelids felt like they had weights on them. He was all over the place and I had a hard time following his Italian. It was too dry for me to handle. When it was over we went around and I met a bunch of people. Next Sunday we are having a party to celebrate my birthday after church so we invited Rose's friends over to join us. Most of them were the same group of friends that we had had gelato with one night a week or so ago. Rose and I left to go downstairs to the bar to get some water and wait for Giosué... he had to put all the gear away.

The rest of the day was very boring and dull. I did the usual- studied, napped, and ate food. The two love birds just napped and had some time together. Later that evening we all went to the dog park. It was a different one than the first one I went to. There were two large, caged in areas that were in the beginning of the park. We chose the area with smaller sized dogs and had a hard time entering through the chain-linked fence gate. We were there for about ten minutes having a nice time when this crazy, curly-haired dude and his husky came along. He freaked us out and we wanted to leave as soon as possible. He would talk and tell these odd stories to no one in particular. He was giving off a funky vibe. Then his damn dog decided to jump up onto my lap with his huge muddy paws. The owner dude didn't even do anything, Giosué had to come help me. It started to get slightly chilly and we walked back home stopping to rent a movie on the history of the mafia. I was too tired to watch it. Rose made a squash soup which I surprisingly liked. I love squash, just not in the soup version, so I thought.

09.06.10

I did it... I made the appointment for my tattoo today!! I can't believe it, now I am about to go through with it, after all these years of planning and dreaming of it. There is a place nearby Rose's apartment called La Burra Tinta and I found it when I was researching parlors in the area. The website was impressive and had photos of the work of the three artists. The difference between the tattooing here and in the States is that there are no regulations on the shops here. No need for certification or sanitation records. I didn't feel like this would be a deal breaker for me, I just knew I wanted to see it before I sat down to have it permanently needled into my skin. So after Rose was finished with her morning lessons we had lunch and off we went to scope out the tattoo parlor. It was tucked in a residential area and felt nice. It was clean and I was comfortable. The first guy we talked to was very nice and asked what I was interested in getting done there. He ended up referring us to his buddy which ended up being the guy I wanted from the pictures I saw of his work online. Simone. How do you do. He was a more handsome version of Ricky Martin. Rose had to be the translator. We set up the appointment for next Thursday at 11 AM. Now it was in writing, in the books. I am so excited about all of this. I am in Italy with my sister about to get a tattoo that's been on my mind for years. Now I have to just figure out how I am going to tell Mom.

With energy and electricity running through my veins we moved on with the rest of our day. Off to SACI we went, Rose was almost done with her most recent sculpture projects. I tried studying, but my brain couldn't focus. Adam came by to say hello. He had a meeting with someone at the school, he wants a job in Italy. I wish I could just get any job or task anywhere and anytime. I feel so constricted when it comes to my career and employment options. I know I can always figure out a way to do something if I really want or find a way around it, but there really are things I just can't do or be. I want to accept that, but does that make me settle for less?

For dinner Rose made a rice and curry coconut chicken. I read more for a bit and started to watch a movie with Rose but went to bed because I had already seen it. I hate watching movies more than once.

09.07.10

I didn't leave the house at all today. Rose didn't have to work until the afternoon so she was getting her new roommate's bedroom all ready and situated. I had to organize and clean up all my stuff I had laying around. She is arriving Thursday, so I will only have two more nights in that room and then I will have to share Rose's room. No big deal, it is just super nice having my own room.

We decided we will go to Udine this Friday afternoon for an overnight stay. The train takes four hours and then we will take a train home late Saturday evening. I am footing the bill for the train tickets, which is not a big deal if that is what it takes for Rose to agree to go with me.

Giosué came over for lunch today...Rose made pasta with fresh tomatoes. I did more studying and reading. The weather was overcast all day. When I woke up this morning it was very foggy out and I couldn't see anything out my window. So, I stayed in my pajamas all day and didn't take a shower until 17h00. When Rose got home we went out for dinner at a restaurant with a ship theme. I had a pizza with mushrooms and zucchini. It was delicious. While we were there Rose and I got into a fight. Poor Giosué was right in the middle of it all watching us go back and forth like a heated tennis match. We were having a disagreement over the Udine trip. She didn't want to go. She was wanting to work on her sculptures more and this trip would hinder that. I stopped the conversation because we were getting to loud and I told her we were done discussing it there and could pick it up later when we got back home. We finished eating and Giosué drove us home in complete silence. It was very awkward, but that is how sisters roll-we love hard and fight hard. I was expecting a spat at some point during my trip and was completely okay with that, it is impossible to not have one when you are around someone all day and night for thirty days. I feel like it shows we are being honest with each other and want get our points across. Nothing wrong with that. When we got back to the apartment I went into my room and studied and read to try and clear my head and figure out the right thing to say to Rose. At one point I got up and went to her room and told her we had to talk at some point that night and that I wasn't going to go to sleep until we talked this out. She eventually came over and told me we were going to be leaving on the 10:30 AM train in two days.

09.08.10

It poured today. Rose had a lesson at the London School, so I went with her. We grabbed a coffee at a bar near the bus stop but had to suck them down because it was about to come. We ended up waiting and waiting. The old lady waiting with us was getting super agitated and complaining the entire time. It ended up that it was just backed up and very packed, I didn't know how Rose and I were going to be able to get through the doors and into the spot reserved for those in wheelchairs. We did it and the people parted for us to get by. There was someone in the spot but they quickly jumped up and got out of our way. As soon as we got on the bus it began to downpour. We missed it by seconds.

We decided to do some shopping after her lesson (the rain had stopped) and went over to Italy's version of a department store. I found some fun socks that I bought with grippy stuff on the bottom shaped as stars. As we were checking out we looked outside and discovered it was raining again. It would have been no big deal, but with a wheelchair and no one else it's nearly impossible to carry an umbrella and hold it up without getting just as soaked as if you didn't have it. We ran to a little sandwich shop that had covered outdoor seating and had lunch, waiting for the rain to stop so that we could go down to SACI and get Rose's sculptures. The food we had was absolutely disgusting, yes it is possible to have gross food in Italy, but when we finished it was still raining so we continued to sit and had a cappuccino. Now that hit the spot, it was so raw out from the rain and the espresso just warmed you right up. When we arrived to Rose's studio we got kicked out by the construction workers there. They were doing who knows what and told us we had to leave for safety reasons. It was a hard hat zone, although they were not wearing hard hats. Oh well, whatever, sometimes it's just not worth questioning men. We left and did what some do best-shopped. We went into one store where in order to get to the bottom floor we had to go out and around through the alleyway and down an extremely steep hill (yes, I thought I was going to topple out so I held on for dear life) and through the garage and their storage room. Unfortunately, it wasn't worth the hike. We went home after that one.

09.09.10

This morning our beautiful weather returned and Rose went out to have breakfast with Giosué. She, as she always is kind enough to think of me, left me with a fabulous cappuccino which I gladly enjoyed on my own on the terrace. The new roommate, Macey, who Rose and I met before we came to Italy, arrived around noon. Rose welcomed her with a lunch of pasta made with olives and mushrooms, it was delicious. Later Rose, Giosué, and Macey went grocery shopping. I packed for Udine, we are going to catch the 10h30 train. My first night sharing a bed with Rose here in Italy!

09.10.10

I'm 26 today! We got up and caught a quick coffee at the bar on the block. We took the bus to SMN and it took so long. The buses seemed to be more backed up than thought possible. It must be the congestion from all the locals coming back into town from their vacations. When we arrived at the train station we went to one of those free standing kiosks where you can buy your ticket on your own and it would not let us get the tickets we needed. We had to do things the old fashioned way and stand in line for a good forty-five minutes. We had to get the next train that didn't leave until 13h30. Rose was a bit upset but more annoyed that our plans were derailed slightly (no pun intended, har har) but I wasn't going to let it ruin our day. It was so nice out and instead of going all the way back to the apartment we called up Adam and met with him at a bar near the train station to have a pastry and coffee. He was up for it so we sat outside at on a nice patio where we could still watch people go by. And since it was so close to the train station most people were frantic or hurried. Better than television. We sat there and chatted for a couple of hours. At one point Rose got up and said she would be right back. And about 45 minutes went by before she actually came back. She had gone to market and was acting a bit shady- trying to keep me from knowing that she went to buy me a gift for my birthday. She even showed Adam what was in the bag and then refused when I asked to see it. It's funny at how horrible she is at lying or keeping a secret. The time had passed us quickly and before we knew it, it was time to go board our train to Udine to see the family I hadn't seen in over twenty years! We bought some sandwiches to take with us to munch on the train when we checked out from the bar.

Our train tickets were for seats not next to each other, but Rose asked a guy in a business suit if we could switch so that we could be next to each other. He gladly got up and we settled into our comfy seats. It was a two hour train ride and then we would have to get off and switch trains. I brought my fabulous travel scrabble and begged Rose to play with me. She did but only because it was my birthday. I beat her pretty badly too. When we were cleaning up the game one of the letters flew out and landed into a black hole in between the seats. Rose's hand was too big to fit in there and my fingers were too short so there is now a tiny scrabble letter floating around in train land in Italy. We had to switch trains in Venezia Statione to a regional train to get us to Udine. Oh man, talk about change of scenery. This train we had to get on was hot as hell, sweaty, and very uncomfortable. The seats were facing each other and so closely that Rose's knees were touching mine. Thankfully, Gigi, our cousin, was there waiting for us when we arrived. I had to pee there and I am not sure why, but we asked the polizia for the bathroom and he radioed someone to unlock the door. A few minutes later four cops and a janitor show up. For some reason, the guy takes us over to the men's room and unlocks the handicapped stall and he told us they keep that one cleaner. Okay, good to know for future requests of bathroom stalls.

We left the station and Gigi only knows Italian and Spanish so I just sat in the back of his mercedes listening to his and Rose's conversation while he took us all over. I felt like I was in Lancaster County, PA again with all the farms and corn fields. It didn't smell like cow crap though, so that kept me on track. It took about twenty minutes to drive to his parent's house (same house as where my grandfather grew up). We went up a skinny graveled lane and there was the house, it felt surreal, all these awesome plants everywhere, including a lime tree, windows wide open, and perfect weather. I felt like I was in Hansel and Gretel for some reason. Houses where I live have character, but not age like this. Our aunt Laura welcomed us with kisses and hugs right when we stepped out of the car. We went into the kitchen and sat around the table to chit chat. I was able to understand and follow about 75% of their conversation which was shocking to me, especially after not having an easy time understanding when Mino was visiting. We had dinner together and it didn't bother my stomach thankfully. Usually if I eat food cooked by someone other than my mom or sisters my stomach becomes a monster. When we were finished Laura had Roberto (Gigi's brother) bring out a fruit tarte with a candle in it for me! We popped a bottle of sparkling wine which went down the drain because it was rancid. Roberto popped another bottle and tested it and seemed to be not 100% sure about it, but we drank it anyway. I had a small glass of it. I wasn't about to get tipsy in my aunt's house. I was so full and tired after all this but we ended up trying to play scrabble with Roberto... in English and/or Italian. Oh man, it was difficult. Rose had advantage of speaking both languages, so she won.

It was pretty late when we finished and I couldn't keep my eyes open any longer. We went upstairs to bed. There were four or five bedrooms. They have wood floors upstairs so you either have to go bare foot or slide/shuffle around on these pieces of cloth. Rose just carried me while she shuffled. I found it very amusing and almost peed my pants before we got to our room. We even had our own bathroom right next to it. There were a bunch of old pictures all around the room of everyone so young including my grandfather, mom, and dad. Rose gave me on of the gifts she had bought me earlier in the day that was from her and Giosué- a sweatshirt with Italia on it. That would come in handy since I didn't bring any sweatshirts and the weather was getting chilly at night!

I had to sleep sans pillow because the one on the bed was so high and puffy my neck wasn't long enough to fit my head comfortably on it. No biggie, I usually end up without a pillow by the end of the night anyway. Pillows are just a pain in the neck, haha, yes, I did it again. Other than that I was comfortable and fell right asleep, even with Rose right next to me on the phone with Giosué.

09.11.10

What a rough morning. I woke up early, whatever time the roosters wake up, to their crowing. Yes, the neighbors have roosters and pigeons. We had ourselves some cooing and crowing. It wasn't a surprise to me though because when I was younger my grandfather had us watch a video he took of a trip to visit his sister and literally videotaped the window and all it was was the noise of the birds for about fifteen minutes. We still joke about that video to this day and now I was experiencing it first hand. So funny. It wasn't so funny though when I had some hot flashes and my heart was racing and felt so nauseated I thought I was gonna puke. I had to get up and go to the bathroom (if you know what I mean) twice before 7:30 AM. Oh that wasn't fun. After the second time I was glued to the toilet I ended up taking a pepto bismal (which I normally enjoy and consider candy) and laid back down hoping all those sick feelings would wash away. I was starting to feel a bit better, but then I moved and it all came right back over me. This time I did puke and didn't stop for the next two hours. I was so embarrassed. I made Rose go down and get me water and open the window to let some cool, fresh air in. She got ready next to me while I just sat on the toilet. Laura ended up making me some hot tea to drink which helped. After that time and the tea I thought I was going to be okay and I was able to get ready and dressed for the day. Well, as soon as I opened the door and the aromas of the foods cooking hit me I had to turn right around and threw up one last time in the toilet. This time I really did feel like it was out of my system. On our way down the stairs we saw Laura and she asked if I was feeling any better and if it was from eating her food. I told her no, of course not, and then she said it must have been because I mixed a glass of red wine with a glass of white wine. I didn't argue. I don't know what made me sick, all I know is that I felt so awful for getting sick there! Rose took me outside to sit and get some fresh air. It felt amazing. I was feeling much better- I was able to admire their plants.

Roberto took Rose and me to the center city of Udine. It is a cute little city on top of a mountain and there is a look out that we went up to and saw all the little houses and Alps in the distance. When we were walking around I smelled some stinky fish and thought it was just in my head since I was sick I thought maybe all smells are rancid right now. But, we turned a corner and there was a huge fresh fish market going on. I couldn't look- it was gross seeing whole fish piled up on top of each other with their heads about to be chopped off. Eventually, we tired of walking around and found a nice place to sit and have a coffee and people watch. We saw a bicycle that was chained up to the railing with a sumo wrestler bell on the handlebar. Some little kid was walking by and saw it and ran up to it to squeeze the sumo's bun, it was pretty amusing. I ordered a shot of espresso because I knew I needed some caffeine in order to make my headache disappear, but I knew if there was anything else (like milk) that it would make me barf again. It worked and I was able to enjoy the day a bit more.

As we were exploring the town I had my camera in my lap. I was getting tired of just holding it up and snapping (I hadn't eaten anything that day so I was a bit shaky) so I just set it on my lap and kept my finger on the shutter button and pushing it randomly hoping to get a few unexpected shots. It worked though and I ended up with a few interesting angles and people and they didn't even know it!

We headed back to the house for lunch. Laura had made pasta with fresh tomatoes. I had a tiny bit with lots of bread and water of course. I was scared to eat too much and have a relapse of the morning. And with having to take the train later it was better to be on the empty side.

We talked for a while and then had some coffee. They have a little neighbor named Sabrina who loves Laura and comes over often to play. She is six years old and calls Laura by the name of Julia. They said when she was a baby she started calling her that and they aren't exactly sure why, but she continued to call her that. She brought a bunch of toys up from her house and was bringing them in. Things like a doll house and it's accessories. She had this bouncing ball that she sat on and just took off like Tiger and all we saw was her head bopping up and down in the kitchen window. She does this frequently. It was very endearing to see her and Laura interact. There is just a great relationship and chemistry that was built between those two and I love to see how Sabrina makes Laura glow and her eyes seem to come alive. It's nice to know that that type of thing exists when it needs to.

Eventually Gigi came over and him and Roberto were going to take us to the train station. We said our goodbyes to Laura, I hoped she enjoyed having us, it was a pleasure and peaceful time there, despite the fact that I got sick. On our way to the station we stopped at three different shoe stores hoping to find me some but we struck out. I guess I will just have to stick with my favorite thing ever- Zappos.com. We still had some time after that so we went to a gelateria. I just played it safe and stuck with the water.

While we were on the loading bin things or whatever they are called, platform I guess, I got super nauseous again and really thought I was going to be sick again. I even started to scope out some nearby trashcans. Luckily it passed after we got on the train. The ride back was nice and uneventful. At our switch in the Venezia Statione we had some extra time before our other train was arriving so we went to the snack back where I found RICE CAKES!!! I love those things, especially when my stomach is off. Rose said she had not seen those ever here in Italy.

When we got on the nice Eurostar train we were sitting across from two little girls, maybe eight-ish. They were hilarious. The one little girl had a sort of bratty air to her and just stared me down like no other. I simply smiled right at her and she would glance away. The other little girl was sweeter about discovering me and would sneak more innocent glances at me. Eventually, they both fell asleep. Rose and I played sudoku the whole way.

Giosué was at the station waiting to pick us up. He was dressed up because we were supposed to go to birthday party for one of their friends. Rose convinced him to drop me off first since I wasn't feeling well. Rose changed and off they went. I don't even know when she got in, I was so tired I was out like a light I guess. Before I went to bed Macey and I hung out a bit. It was nice to talk with her and see how she was feeling after being in a foreign country for two days. I knew what it was like to be in her shoes and she couldn't get her internet to work so I let her use my camera and signed her onto the internet so she could skype with her parents. I unpacked and showered because I knew I wouldn't want to get up early to do that and we had church the next morning.

09.12.10

Giosué picked us up around 9 AM for church. Macey came along with us. We once again had a coffee and pastry before the service began while Giosué was setting up sound and video. Davide led worship with much energy and enthusiasm. It was interesting because 75% of the songs we sang I knew from my middle school days at a Christian school. Since they were in Italian, they were only familiar in tune and I was able to rediscover and reconnect with the actual meaning of the songs. Then, Andre, Davide's older brother, spoke about the parable of the seed. I understood more than the last service we went to, but I kept catching myself spacing out. We met a bunch of new people after the service but had to leave quickly because Giosué was going to be late for work and he had to drop us off first. Rose picked us up some sandwiches to have for lunch. We just hung around for the rest of the afternoon. My request for the birthday meal was chili and Rose even whipped up some cornbread to go with it for later that evening. I was excited to have a small gathering at Rose's apartment with 80% of our guests all speaking a bit of English. We ended up having eleven people over and we just pulled all the tables together and had a great time eating and chatting. Rose then made me open presents in front of everyone which I tried to refuse to do because I find that sort of thing quite embarrassing. Believe it or not, I really don't enjoy being the center of attention like that. My face and ears were burning bright red while I opened the gifts. They were very nice though, Rose bought me some glass earrings and a leather purse I really wanted from the market. Macey wrote me a very sweet card (which I read later) and the rest of the gang gave me a leather-bound journal (a girl can never have too many of those!). Adam made a small painting for me with a fleur de lis and New Jersey...to incorporate those things together takes talent. We ended the night by going to get gelato. We were all going to walk there, but a few people were huffing about it and we ended up piling into three different cars to get there.

09.13.10

It rained this afternoon and evening. I did basically nothing. I finished another book and studied. Rose made pasta for lunch and a delicious pot roast for dinner. She worked on sculpting and I watched and drank a huge mug of Earl Grey tea which made me get up every fifteen minutes to pee. We worked on my tattoo design. It isn't quite where I want it, but it's almost there. I want it to have strong, solid lines but also flowy and sketchy. I am going to ask the tattoo artist to look at all the different drawings that Rose and Darcey created and see if he can merge them and draw something that has a bit of everything in it.

09.14.10

Rose was going to be teaching her ceramics students today and I was going to go with her but this morning was feeling tired and nauseous which made me want to stay home, but at the last moment Rose convinced me to change my mind and I got ready in fifteen minutes. We grabbed the 17 bus to SMN train station. This took forever and was making me feel even sicker. I had to make myself look out the window and up at the sky (when there weren't thousand of year old buildings blocking the way) and pretend like I had all the space in the world- that is my trick that my mom use to have us do when we got car sick. It at least helped me not to puke. We jumped off the bus and Rose was running while pushing me in my wheelchair, which is always a scary thing no matter who is doing the pushing. I just threaten whoever is tsk tsking me for freaking out that when they are old and in a wheelchair I will pay the attendant to give them a quicker shove than normal and see how they like it. That tactic rarely works, but I have to try something to get them to realize that it is a scary thing to have no control over the speed and if I hit a bump I don't know whether or not I will catapult out and onto the ground until I am already there. Rose understands this because a few years back she was pushing me and I freaked out at her telling her she was making me nervous that I was going to be flat on my face and she told me I was overreacting and the next moment what do you know, we hit a minuscule bump that even I didn't see and I was flying through the air. I tried catching myself but that didn't work and I ended up with a gash in my knee. There is still a slight scar there that I enjoy pointing out to Rose... I find it humorous, but she definitely does not. Anyway, she saw that I was uncomfortable with the speed we were traveling from the station to the university so she slowed down a bit for me. When we got to SACI I sat in the courtyard and tried to study. Thankfully, I was at least starting to feel better as I was munching bread-sticks I brought along. Adam came to hang out a bit too, he was leaving in a few days to travel around in Europe. The first class was finished at noon so Rose, Adam, Lisa (the professor), and I went together to our favorite sandwich shop to have lunch. After eating and before

Rose had to help with the next class we headed over to one of the stores that Rose bought her purse from to complain because the color was fading in an unnatural way and she thought it might be a knock-off. Her and the store clerk went at it for a good half hour and in the end the woman took the purse back and said they would give her another one. While that was going on Adam and I amused ourselves in the store. Once it was all done and over with Rose and I had to get back to her class and we said our goodbyes to Adam. On the way we stopped for a quick pick-us-up coffee. I love that about Italy.

After the class was finished we tried shopping but it was very unsuccessful and it was starting to get super annoying so we gave up. I was over it. We wanted to buy belts for five euros in the market like we did a few years ago, but the problem was that that was a few years ago, now they barely will go for fifteen euros. We were hungry and tired so we sat down at a bar where I had a tea and pastry with chocolate and Rose just had a coffee. When I ordered my tea without lemon or milk the guy thought I was crazy and asked where I was from and then asked, "Ohio?". Wrong buddy. I don't think there is a more random state than that.

We picked up two sculptures to take home with us and they both were half of my weight, each. One was on my lap and then tied around and behind me. Rose managed to get the other one on her hip. We were on the bus during a rush hour-ish time too so we didn't have much room to move around in. We made it and were drenched in sweat by the time we got through her apartment door.

09.15.10

Tomorrow I get my tattoo finally! I am so excited and it's all I can think about. Besides what I am going to tell my mom. I think it is a great way to end my adventure here.

Another day of gorgeous weather. I was up at 7:30 AM because Rose has lessons until after lunch and she made me a coffee before she headed out. I was just painting some bananas. I needed a break from studying the GMAT stuff. And I was able to eat one when I was finished. At 15h30 Giosué and his younger brother came by to pick us up. Oscar had a piano audition up in Fiesolé at a music high school conservatory. The roads to get there were so narrow and scary I had to close my eyes on the way there. While he did his thing we hung out and sat in the grass outside the building he was in. The mosquitoes were bad there and the sun was going down so they were getting worse. To celebrate his being finished with the audition we stopped at Badiani (the same gelateria we always love going to) and had our dessert before dinner. Since my stomach was still not feeling the gelato I opted for a cornetto with nutella in the middle, definitely not a food to eat when on a date.

09.16.10

It's DONE!!! My left arm now has a beautiful, permanent art piece. I am still in complete shock and cannot believe I am staring at my new tattoo! It went awesomely.

I woke up so excited and nervous. We were running behind because I dropped a glass of water and it shattered all over the place. Rose had to clean it up so that Pina wouldn't step on any of the pieces. And then as usual, bus 17 was running late. We were able to text Simone to let him know we were on the way and he replied: no problem. When we got off the bus we made a quick pit stop a a bar to get a coffee since we were already late. The weather was very overcast, but it didn't rain and later the sun came out for a visit. We got to the tattoo parlor and I was becoming more and more anxious to get it done. We gave Simone a few of the sketches we had been working on and he drew a beautiful fleur de lis that was better than I could have imagined. It was bigger than what I was thinking but it was perfect and it didn't need any changes made to it, including the size, that was part of the beauty of it. He went back to his station/room to set things up and in the meantime I popped a few extra of my medicine to keep my nerve pain in check. He led us back and I just took my left arm out of my shirt and laid on the table. He had an arm rest contraption like the ones they use in the operation room to put your arm with the IV on. I let my arm relax on the thing and we began. He didn't shave the area of my arm, but wiped it with some sort of solution and then put the drawing on my arm. It was awesome. Off he went with the needle. It didn't hurt, just felt weird. My right arm though was twitching and spasming in reaction. I had Rose hold my shoulder and hand down so that it wouldn't make the rest of my body move. He did the outline first and had to switch needles to do the shading. He asked me if I needed a break and I didn't so we kept on cruising. And just like that it was finished. He cleaned up the area of the ink and blood and put a layer of vaseline over it. On top of that he put a piece of saran wrap which he told me to keep on for three hours. I was told to wash it with sensitive soap four to five times a day. It can't be exposed to the sun, pool, or ocean for forty days. We got our picture together and then Rose and I were off.

We stopped for lunch and the lady didn't even bring us what we ordered and argued with Rose when she told her. I ended up having penne with a hazelnut cream sauce. When we were leaving these two old guys with English accents were trying to get us to have a conversation with them. One of them basically proposed to Rose, said he loved her and would get a rose of sharon tattooed on his arm. We left them as quickly as possible and went home because Rose had to go back to work to teach. I just hung around the apartment- took a nap and sat out on the terrace. The rest of the evening was easy going. We got some groceries and a movie and went to bed.

09.17.10

It has been thirty days in Italy. It's packing day. The weather reflects my mood- rainy and miserable. I laid around and thought about packing mostly. I did everything I could but that. I put pictures from my camera onto a hard drive for Rose (I took over one thousand photos- I hope there are a few good ones in there). I was able to skype Mick to show her my tattoo and she was speechless. Shocked by the size of it. I ended up handwriting Rose a letter to thank her for all she had done for me while I stayed here and to remind her why I love her so much. It took me a very long time to write it and I had to take a break in between. I am going to give it to Giosué to give it to her after I am dropped off at the airport tomorrow. That afternoon Rose, Giosué, Pina and I took a walk in the rain. I had to get some fresh air and it wasn't pouring or anything so it wasn't bad. We were a tad bit wet by the end of it but well worth getting outside. For my last supper we chose to have a pizza at the place around the corner where we had Darcey's last dinner in Italy. We made reservations for 20h00. Macey came along with us as well. We were having a nice time but Giosué had to leave early to go to work, he is filming at a club for a promo of theirs. We stayed and chatted since it was a Friday evening and we had no other plans. After we left the pizzeria I needed to get some cash from the ATM so I could repay Rose for money she let me use for my tattoo and give her extra for groceries. When we got to the ATM I couldn't find my debit card and we had to go home and basically unpack my whole suitcase to find it in the pocket of my pants. At least we found it. Rose and I went to bed at a decent hour because Giosué was picking us up at 8 AM. We watched Julie and Julia. I of course fell asleep while we watched it.

09.18.10

We checked my bags with no issues and I was ushered away by a random worker dude carrying his purse and constantly checking his phone. We got to the security area and were waiting in line and that is where Rose and Giosué had to stop. The guy wouldn't let them go any further so Rose came to hug and kiss me goodbye and the people in line behind me got all huffy puffy because we were holding the line up. This made Rose even more upset, but I managed to distract myself enough not to cry. I had given Giosué the letter to give to her when they got back to the car so I felt okay with the quick, interrupted goodbye. I began my journey home. Back to my boring and crazy life in my tiny town where I had no job, car, or anything else. But I couldn't wait to get back to it. I can love more than one way of living. Italy is fabulous, but so is Lititz. They are incomparable. Don't even bother to ask me the question which I like better. That is a stupid question, and if you ask anyone I know they will tell you I really hate stupid questions.

10 FINAL THOUGHT

This whole experience is teaching me to be passionately patient. I am not one to have patience, it's always something I've struggled with and need more of (an ability or willingness to suppress restlessness or annoyance when confronted with delay). There is a time for everything and I have to learn to accept that and keep in mind that I do have a purpose and I was made to succeed. It's easy to forget lessons learned and dwell too much on the one you're currently facing and fear the ones to come. In Romans 5:3-5 it says, "There's more to come: We continue to shout our praise even when we're hemmed in with troubles, because we know how troubles can develop passionate patience in us, and how that patience in turn forges the tempered steel of virtue, keeping us alert for whatever God will do next. In alert expectancy such as this, we're never left feeling shortchanged. Quite the contrary—we can't round up enough containers to hold everything God generously pours into our lives through the Holy Spirit!"

Although this experience has changed my whole future and where I thought I was heading with my life, it's reminded me of what is important and appreciating the things in life that are often taken for granted. I can do anything through Christ who strengthens me. I have determination. I have a purpose. I will overcome.